SELINA LAKE
Outdoor Living

SELINA LAKE
Outdoor Living

AN INSPIRATIONAL GUIDE TO MAKING THE MOST
OF YOUR OUTDOOR SPACES

with photography
by Debi Treloar

RYLAND PETERS & SMALL
LONDON • NEW YORK

TEXT AND STYLING Selina Lake
SENIOR DESIGNER Barbara Zuñiga
SENIOR COMMISSIONING EDITOR Annabel Morgan
COMMISSIONING EDITOR Nathan Joyce
LOCATION RESEARCH Selina Lake and Jess Walton
HEAD OF PRODUCTION Patricia Harrington
PRODUCTION Silvia La Greca
ART DIRECTOR Leslie Harrington
EDITORIAL DIRECTOR Julia Charles

First published in 2014
By **Ryland Peters & Small**
20–21 Jockey's Fields
London WC1R 4BW
and
519 Broadway, 5th Floor
New York, NY 10012
www.rylandpeters.com

Text copyright © Selina Lake 2014
Design and photographs copyright
© Ryland Peters & Small 2014

10 9 8 7 6 5 4 3 2 1

ISBN 978-1-84975-506-1

A CIP record for this book is available from the British
Library.

Library of Congress CIP data has been applied for.

Printed and bound in China

CONTENTS

INTRODUCTION

I've really loved bringing my signature fresh, pretty and vintage style to outdoor spaces! In this book, I show you my style tips for creating amazing garden parties, picnics and barn dances with handy hints for you to recreate some of my ideas at home or in outside spaces that you have access to.

My fondest childhood memories are of the summers I spent outside in my parents' garden playing with my sister under the sprinkler, enjoying picnics with my family at Windsor Great Park and blustery walks along the promenade while visiting my grandparents by the sea. For me there is nothing better than spending the day outside in the fresh air soaking up the atmosphere.

I really enjoyed the freedom of styling outside spaces. There are not as many restrictions as there are inside and there are plenty of opportunities to try new things and most of all have fun! I like to be quite crafty with my styling ideas and make my own decorations, lighting ideas and textiles, so if you want to have a go at some of my DIY ideas look for the *Here's How* sections in the book. Have fun embracing the magic of styling your outside space!

OPPOSITE David Austin Rose Garden in Wolverhampton, UK is a magical place to visit when the roses are in full bloom. I love the horseshoe shield with hooks, which I picked up at my local charity shop. It's an ideal place to hang flowers and worked perfectly as part of the decor for my barn dance party.

THIS PAGE This tent's deck is the perfect place to relax — from here you have access to stunning Cornish views. These cute little jars of honey with easy-to-make vintage floral fabric lids are a great gift for your guests to take home with them as a wedding favour or just as part of a party bag!

INSPIRATIONS

Summer dining in buttercup heaven. How could this magical setting not inspire you? We are lucky to live in a world with many stunning natural beauty spots – lakes, country gardens, city rooftops with amazing views, and fields filled with wild flowers, such as buttercups, poppies and lavender – all of which encourage me to create appealing spaces to eat, relax and entertain outside.

I felt completely inspired running around this gorgeous field of buttercups on a perfect summer's day in the countryside and, of course, I donned my floral dress for the occasion. Beautiful fresh flowers are my favourite styling prop because they instantly enhance any setting as well as adding colour and scent. Summer is when some of my best-loved blooms are in abundance – lilacs, sweet peas, hydrangeas, stocks, peonies and, especially, fragrant David Austin Roses. I like to make loose posies, which I think look more dreamy and romantic than tightly bunched bouquets.

VINTAGE CHINA

One of my greatest passions is collecting vintage china. I buy second-hand plates, teacups, teapots and jugs/pitchers from charity shops and vintage fairs. I'm always drawn to items with floral patterns and if there is a hint of gilding, then it's definitely the piece I'm buying! Instead of saving it for special occasions, I use my vintage china every day. Don't be afraid to take some of your favourite pieces outside – pretty vintage plates laid out on a garden table are a real delight. Add a few jam jars filled with flowers and your table will instantly become a beautiful place to have dinner.

BRINGING THE INSIDE OUT

I love this vintage armchair upholstered in mustard-coloured velvet. It may not be the most practical chair to use outside, but doesn't it look stunning sitting amongst the buttercups with this posy of vibrant blooms resting against the arm? Styling an area outside, whether it be for relaxing or holding a flower-filled vintage tea party, is all about creating a space that both looks and feels inviting. I find that dragging an indoor armchair outside into a beautiful floral setting on a sunny day fills me with genuine happiness. Look around your home and see what 'indoor' pieces you own that would work outside next time the weather is on your side.

ROMANTIC BREAKFAST

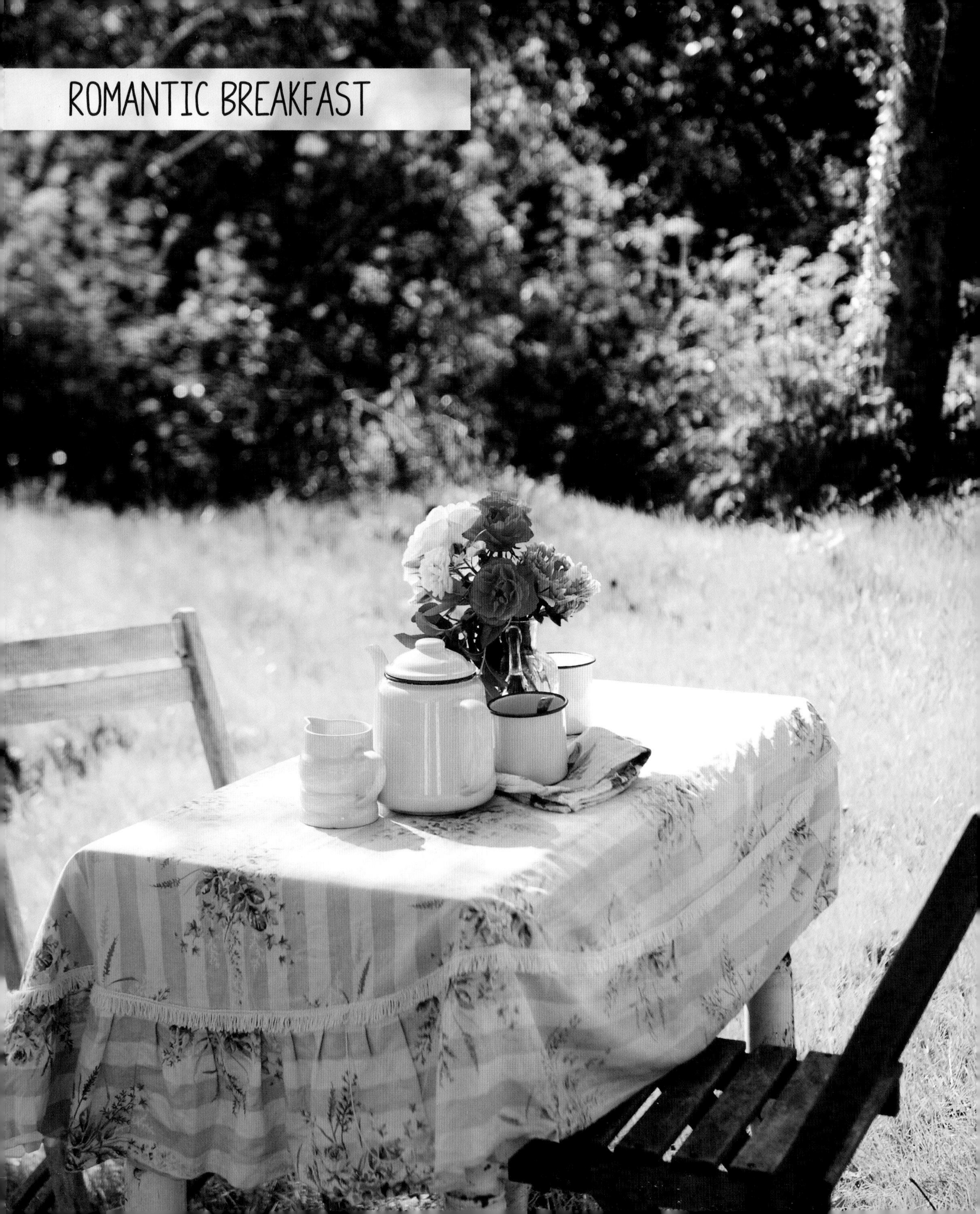

A small table and two mismatched chairs have
been brought together to make a sweet little spot
for a romantic breakfast. I enjoy nothing more
than eating breakfast outside, so whenever it's
a beautiful day, I can hardly lay the table quickly
enough. I bought this vintage floral tablecloth
especially for my wedding reception and I love
to get it out from time to time to brighten up my
garden table. Pastel-coloured enamelware by
Falconware suits the laid-back mood of
breakfasting outside and, of course, pretty
bunting has been inspiring folk for generations
and is such a versatile styling tool.

Outside as well as in, mirrors create an illusion of more light and space, and reflect pretty trees, foliage and flowers. I've bought several Art Deco mirrors from vintage fairs, as I adore the etched-glass patterns, curved shapes and bevelled edges. Mirrors like this make a statement when hung in groups and often look even better with a bit of weathering.

INSPIRATION BOARDS

Making a collage of images, colour swatches and fabrics helps to consolidate ideas, and if a theme works well as a board, it will often translate well for the event or room you're working on. I simply stick postcards, watercolours and seed packets to a wall using washi tape. I also hammer in picture tacks so I can hang decorations, ribbons or posies of flowers.

ECLECTIC SEATING

Seating areas are essential for entertaining and relaxing, even in the smallest outdoor spaces. Old deck chairs, wooden benches and wrought-iron chairs turn up regularly at flea markets and vintage sales. Try mixing such pieces with new finds from home and garden superstores. I teamed jazzy orange and pink metal armchairs from IKEA with French-style garden chairs, a quirky stool and a painted wooden table. The floral cushions and orange jug/pitcher of hydrangeas complete this eclectic outside lounge.

INSPIRATION BOARDS

THIS PAGE Are you looking for inspiration about how to display some of your home-grown flowers? Perhaps you could use some vintage teacups to set off a pretty little posy, like I've done here with this wonderful purple primrose next to a handful of bright butercups

Think of your outside space as an extension of your home, and whatever inspired your design choices inside can also be the springboard for an outdoors scheme. If you have space, a cabin or a summerhouse can be a wonderful addition to a garden. Try decorating its walls with your inspiration boards, which are not only a useful way to record ideas and formulate designs, but are also a lovely way to add colour and pattern to your garden room, potting shed or cabin.

INSPIRATION IS ALL AROUND YOU

Next time you are out and about, keep a lookout for things that inspire you. Perhaps the pink of a budding rose might be the perfect shade to paint your shed. Maybe you will see something unusual in a vintage shop that would look great in your garden, or find a second-hand basket that would make an ideal picnic hamper. When you head out for the day, pack up a picnic and a rug or a couple of deck chairs, so if you chance upon a beautiful spot you will be ready to park up for a while and enjoy the outdoors.

OUTDOOR LIVING

GARDENS

You don't have to be an expert gardener to achieve my style outside, you just need lots of colourful and pretty accessories, and to look at what you have in a different light. Could your old potting shed be transformed into a garden hideaway, or how about assembling a makeshift table using old wooden pallets? On the following pages are ideas for making garden lights and scented sachets, as well as whimsical style tips for using flowers from the garden in romantic ways. Whatever outdoor space you have, make the most of it and enjoy living outside!

MY STYLE TIPS:

* Seating is an all-important factor in a garden that is to be used for relaxing. For an alternative to popular rattan sofas you could commission a carpenter to build a custom-made seating area to suit your space. This one, made from old scaffolding boards, incorporates a place to plant some greenery and a handy cache under the seats to store the seat pads and cushions at night or in the winter. It has been designed in a sociable horseshoe shape and sits on a wooden deck at the bottom of the garden.

* The foam seat pads have been covered loosely, simply by wrapping white vintage lace tablecloths around them. I love the freedom of using textiles outside – you never have to worry about ironing, as the creases and wrinkles add a lived-in charm to a seating area.

* A waterproof woven sail canopy not only provides shade over the outdoor lounge, but it also means the area can be enjoyed even if it starts to drizzle.

* When you serve guests drinks, it's essential that they have a place to put down their glasses. So, if you don't have a designated garden coffee table, carry your living room one outside or invest in a handy stool, which can double as a garden side table. If you have a small table that doesn't match the theme of your outside space, use some vintage fabric as a tablecloth to cover it.

* Add an extra flash of colour with a home-made garland of neon stars. I simply threaded some tiny neon card stars, which I bought from a stationery shop, onto a length of cotton, knotting it on either side of each star to stop them from slipping and bunching up. I love how the neon pops against the vivid green backdrop.

THIS PAGE Most of us like to relax and unwind in our leisure time and, for me, not much could be better than reclining on a bed of throws and cushions in the open air on a lovely sunny day. For the ultimate in summer indulgence, drag a bed into the garden. A simple wooden bench can become a cosy place to sit and read if you add a couple of comfy cushions, while a floral sun lounger from Cath Kidston makes a pretty spot from which to enjoy your garden. OPPOSITE A French metal daybed makes a dreamy place to recline and listen to the radio – just remember to bring the cushions and bedding inside if it starts to rain.

THIS PAGE AND OPPOSITE Let a patch of lawn in your garden become a little overgrown and wild. It could make the perfect spot on which to stretch out in the sunshine – just grab a blanket and some cushions and you are ready to do some serious lounging.

Constructing a wooden shelter over a bench seat enables you to enjoy your garden even on days when the weather is not so good. it's particularly beautiful surrounded by fragrant climbing roses.

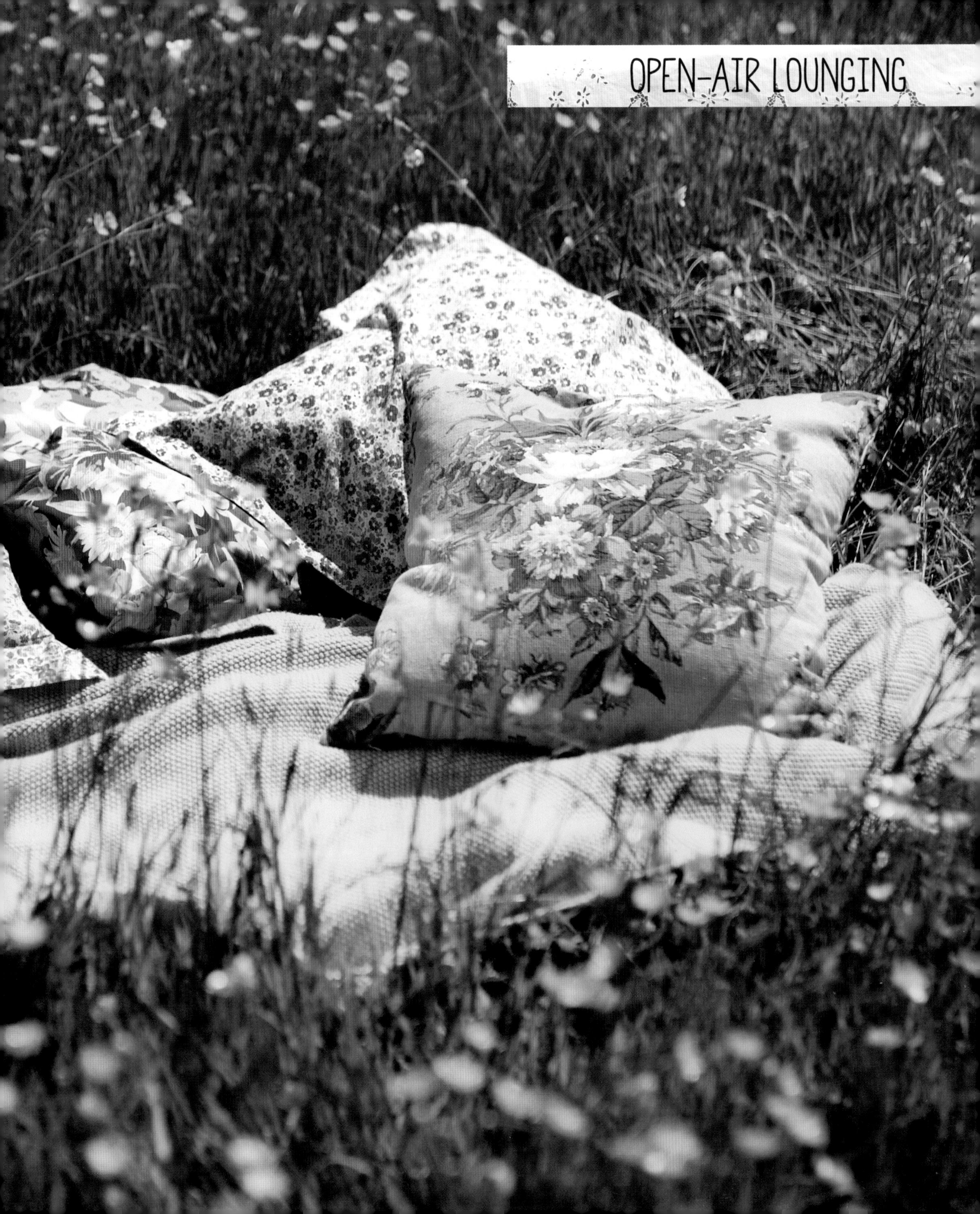

In the summer, I ♥ pre-dinner drinks and nibbles on the deck....

THIS PAGE AND OPPOSITE A modern outside dining area has been set up on this wooden deck under a canopy of tropical greenery that creates a feeling of intimacy. The zesty lemon, lime, vibrant orange and hot pink garden chairs accentuate the tropical vibe of this urban garden. The Oriental-inspired vase holding delicate sprigs from the garden adds a pretty touch to the table, where drinks and olives have been laid out ready to be enjoyed before dinner.

MY STYLE TIPS:

* If your deck leads straight out from your home, think about painting it the same colour as your floor inside for a pleasing sense of continuation. For a fresh Scandinavian look, I'm a fan of white-painted floorboards continuing onto the deck outside. Decks can also look super-stylish painted black. You could also use pastel colours to create a candy-striped or chequerboard effect, or use floor stencils to paint pretty patterns. Remember to use exterior paint for wood and follow the manufacturer's instructions.

* Pots of plants are handy on terraces, decks and patios as they can be moved around at will and are easier to manage than flowerbeds. I love buying old terracotta pots from vintage fairs and markets. Think about reinventing unusual items as planters, too. I reused an old galvanized bathtub as a planter for herbs in my garden. I simply drilled a few holes in the bottom for drainage, added an even layer of stones and pebbles across the base, and then filled it with soil. I bought rosemary, thyme, dill and sage plants from a garden centre and made space to plant them across the filled tub. Mint is notorious for spreading like wildfire, so I planted some separately in an old galvanized bucket, which I picked up from a flea market.

* To make your decking area feel like a cosy living space, bring out a rug or woven mat to place between a couple of chairs, add a coffee table and a vase of fresh flowers and you will have instantly created a garden lounge to sit in and enjoy.

THIS PAGE AND OPPOSITE Both of these terraces have rusty elements in common, which always look appealing in an outdoor setting. If you have a wooden deck or terrace area in your garden, think about how you could incorporate other materials and textures, such as by introducing a metal divider to separate areas of your garden into different zones.

On this page, an old brick wall becomes the perfect background for this rusty metal table and wooden slatted chairs. Don't worry if you have a selection of chairs that aren't all the same, as the mix-and-match approach adds an eclectic element to an outside space. A string of fabric bunting nicely counteracts the hardness of the brick wall.

On the opposite page, I've used old crates as impromptu coffee tables. These small-scale chairs and little crate are ideal for a children's tea party. Behind them, the effect of the rusty wall has been softened by hanging a handmade wreath of foliage and flowers from a pretty ribbon.

THIS PAGE Summerhouses have been enjoyed by everyone from famous writers, who have created their best works in the quiet tranquillity of a garden, to the mandarins of ancient China, who would retreat to their summerhouses to seek inspiration and wisdom from the natural surroundings. A summerhouse makes a great addition to a garden and could provide a guest room, crafting studio, home office or playroom. They can be bought as kits, which you assemble yourself, or you could commission a carpenter or builder to put one together to your own design. Painting the floor, walls and ceiling pure-white will make your space appear bigger and give it a serene feel.

THIS PAGE As long as your
summerhouse is weatherproof,
treat it as you would an inside
space and use comfy chairs and
furniture and furnishings from
inside. If your summerhouse has
electricity and running water, add
a kettle and a mini refrigerator
so you can make cups of tea and
keep drinks cool. Retro 1950s
kitchen dressers/hutches make
ideal storage units.

GARDEN LIGHTING

MY STYLE TIPS:

* Arranging lanterns up a flight of steps or along a path is a lovely way to add some light to a dark spot and is especially nice for garden parties.

* Vintage glassware is the perfect vessel for tea lights. I bought this basket of cut glass from my local charity shop for a fraction of the cost of new glass bowls and jugs/pitchers, and candles look amazing in them, as the light bounces off all the facets. Group a selection together to create a striking centrepiece.

* I love the idea of using apples as tea-light holders. You will need a sharp knife and a steady hand to carve out a space for the tea lights to fit. This method works with most fruit and vegetables. You could also use tapered candles instead of tea lights.

I ♡ candlelight flickering against cut glass...

* Filling an old bathtub, metal bucket or ceramic butler's sink with water, floating candles and flower heads is a sweet and inexpensive lighting feature for parties or evening gatherings in the garden. You could also try this idea on a smaller scale by filling jam jars with water and floating a candle and a few daisies in each one.

* Festoon lights – 1950s-style strings of light bulbs, which are typically found at funfairs, festivals and the seaside – make perfect party lights. They can be strung between posts, draped over the branches of a tree or across a house or shed for a decorative and practical effect. I used the ones on the opposite page at my wedding and love the soft points of light they create. For a different look, you could add paper lanterns to shade the naked bulbs.

* Solar-powered fairy lights are a great addition to any garden; they simply light up when the sun goes down, without the need to plug them in or switch them on. Here I arranged a string of lights around my collection of old galvanized buckets and watering cans to turn them into even more of a feature. Solar-powered fairy lights also look magical twinkling in bushes and hanging along fences.

* I've always thought that rusty lanterns have a certain charm. If you agree, leave your metal lanterns outside (except the stainless steel ones) to brave the elements and eventually rust will start to appear.

IDEAS FOR LIGHTING

HERE'S HOW: *Glass Jar Lanterns*

* To make these little beauties, you need some clean glass food jars, scraps of patterned wallpaper, giftwrap or fabric, PVA glue, a glue brush and plasticized raffia.

* Start by cutting squares of wallpaper, giftwrap or fabric. Glue them around the jar in a patchwork effect, leaving a band of clear glass at the top. Tie a piece of raffia securely around the rim of the jar and then attach another length of raffia to it on both sides so the lantern can be hung up.

* Pop a tealight or a small candle inside and find a branch to suspend the jar from.

I ♡ these patchwork glass jar lanterns...

48

Strings of lights hanging in the branches of trees look magical...

HERE'S HOW: *Lampshade Garland*

✳ These mini lampshades were handmade with vintage bark-cloth fabrics by Folly & Glee. You can create similar ones using a mix of old and new small shades.

✳ Tie the lampshades onto a length of ribbon or cord, leaving an equal space between each one. Tie the ends of the garland securely to the branches of a tree and then thread a string of fairy lights through the shades. I used solar-powered string lights in order to avoid trailing lengths of cables across the lawn.

A mix of vintage floral textiles looks wonderful in the garden...

I ♥ dappled sunlight...

THIS PAGE AND OPPOSITE There's something special about relaxing outside. Perhaps it's the fresh air and surrounding nature that encourages us to take time out and simply laze. If, like me, you enjoy buying and collecting vintage eiderdowns and quilts, then why not create a comfy patchwork seating area on the ground as a fun way to use them in the summer months, when it's too hot to adorn beds with them. The best thing about creating a lounging space such as this is that there is always room to add more throws or blankets as friends and family arrive.

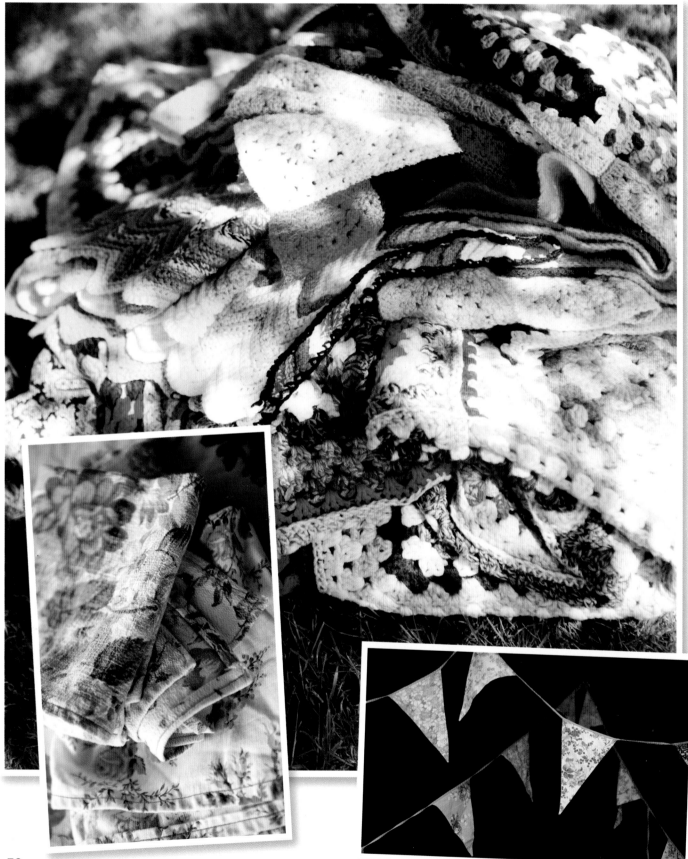

THIS PAGE AND OPPOSITE
Textiles are a quick and fairly inexpensive way to give your outside space some style. Who doesn't love a string of vintage floral bunting gently fluttering in the breeze? There are many other ways textiles can enhance your space. Cushions instantly transform hard chairs into comfy seats, while crocheted blankets give furniture a homespun makeover and are great for wrapping up in when the sun goes down. I like using vintage fabric as tablecloths and sewing my own napkins for special al fresco dining occasions. I made almost 100 napkins for my wedding reception in a mix of my favourite floral fabrics. Simply cut out squares of fabric and iron a rolled hem along each edge before stitching it in place. If you are not a keen sewer, use pinking shears to cut out the napkins – then there is no need for sewing.

MY STYLE TIPS:

* Potting sheds have a rustic charm and I find them to be very inspiring little spaces. My grandmother was a keen gardener and her potting shed at the bottom of her garden always had so many lovely things on display – such as pretty china mugs, at the ready for her morning coffee to be poured from her flask, an array of beautifully illustrated seed packets and lovely old wicker baskets. Do you have a potting shed that could double as a space to sit, think and be inspired?

* Soften the appearance of new wooden gates, fences and metal door bolts by painting them in subtle earthy green tones using exterior paint.

* An attractive a rusty bird feeder hanging from a branch doubles as a flower and candle holder. Beautiful birdhouses and feeders such as this can be bought from specialist garden antiques dealers.

* I absolutely love vintage terracotta plant pots – the more weathered and mossy, the better! They look so sweet planted with pretty pink geraniums or a selection of herbs to create a kitchen garden. You will often find them when you are out-and-about at fairs and flea markets. Keep a look-out for vintage seed packets, too, as they usually feature beautiful designs that make them worth framing.

* Sometimes the smallest details can make a big different to the look and feel of a space. This garden hose was once a typical garish yellow, but a lick of soft green exterior paint makes it blend in with the plants.

THIS PAGE This decorative antique white metal rocking chair is the perfect addition to this pretty porch, where ivy has been left to grow and weave itself between the railings. If you are looking for a similar piece, check out your local antiques fairs, vintage markets and second-hand shops or on-line auction sites. The little lanterns hanging from the porch railing add a whimsical glow.

HERE'S HOW: *Floral Swing*

✳ You will need some freshly cut flowers to adorn your swing. I used lilac, which was plentiful in my garden at the time, and bound the stems to the rope securely using string wire. Remember to leave a section of the rope clear so that you can hold on when sitting on the swing without crushing the delicate flowers.

✳ To add to the prettiness, I folded a small lace tablecloth over the seat. You could also add a cushion for extra comfort.

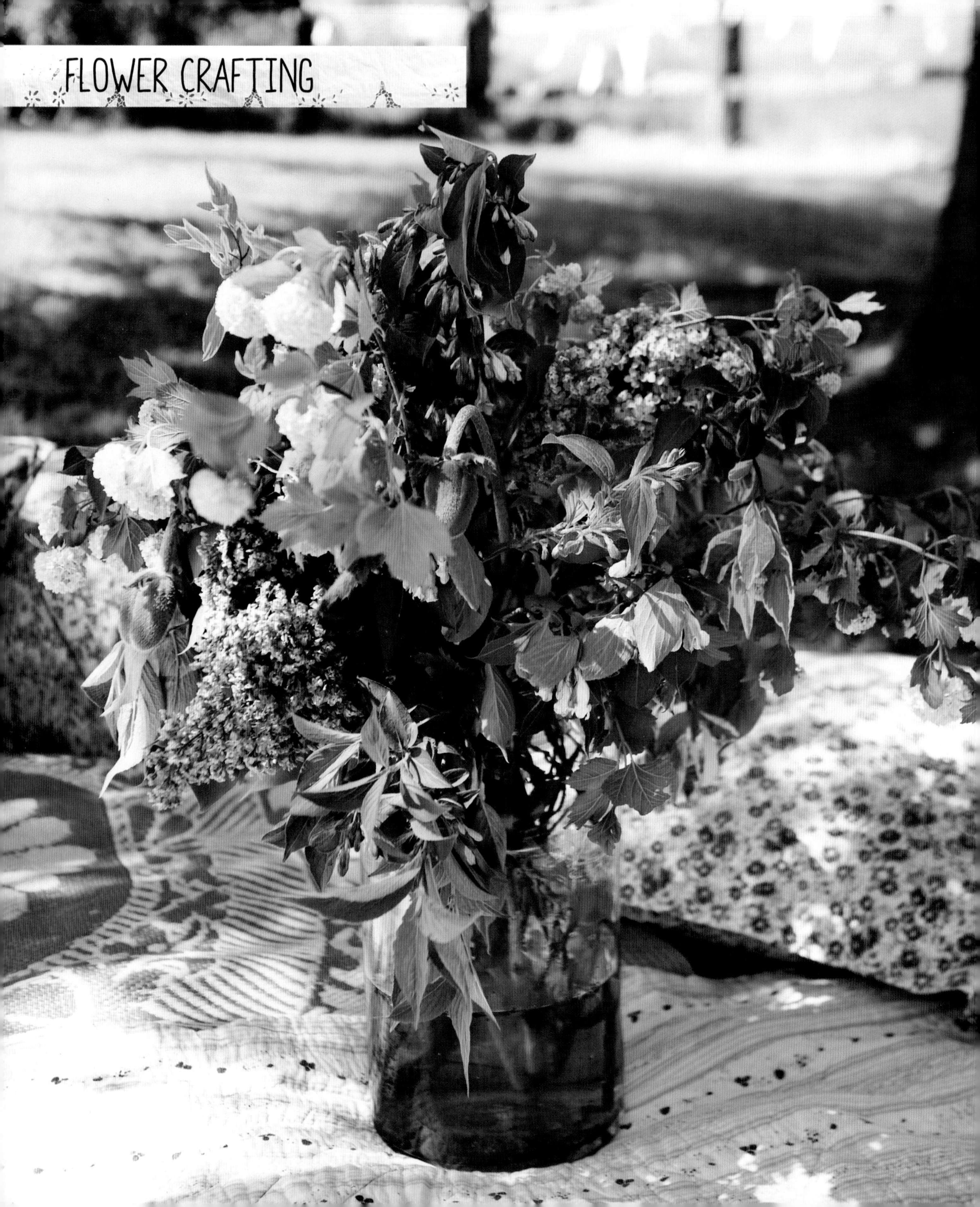

MY STYLE TIPS:

* My favourite vessels for flowers are recycled jam jars, which come in a variety of sizes and styles. Wash the empty jar well and soak it to remove the label, then half-fill it with fresh cold water and arrange your flowers.

* Make your own bouquets and posies using cuttings from your garden. When you prune back any flowering plants, save the cuttings and display them in a large jug/pitcher, vase or bucket.

* Try growing your own blooms to make a statement. This vase of home-grown royal-blue delphiniums is stunning. Cut flower stems at an angle and change the water after a couple of days.

* I often buy vintage books on flowers and gardening from second-hand bookshops and antiques fairs. I love the cover design of this one. If any pages are loose, I take them out and use them as wall art or for a collage.

HERE'S HOW: *Floral Hair Garland*

✱ You will need some pretty flowers with stems cut to around 2 cm (¾ inch). I used a mix of the most fragrant David Austin Roses I could find. I used rustic string wire from a garden centre for the band and craft wire to attach the flowers.

✱ Measure around your head and cut the string wire to size, leaving a little extra to wind the ends together and to allow space for the flowers. Secure the stems onto the band by wrapping them together with craft wire. When the band is full of blooms, fill in any gaps with leaves.

THIS PAGE I love antique flower books, which often feature beautifully painted, inspirational illustrations – they often give me ideas for floral decorations for parties or special occasions. If you have an abundance of flowers in your garden in the summer months, think of other ways that you could enjoy them. Take inspiration from vintage flower books for different varieties to grow for next summer, too. You could use the same method as the Floral Hair Garland, opposite, to make a wreath to hang on a gate or fence, or simply lay flower heads on the ground in the shape of a heart to surprise someone you love (see page 27). You could create a similar effect using leaves or tea lights.

I ♡ gathering flowers
from the garden...

LAUNDRY DAY

I ♡ pretty washing lines...

*There's something magical about
clean washing drying in the breeze...*

THIS PAGE AND OPPOSITE Whenever I buy old
pieces of floral fabric or vintage linens,
I can't wait to get them washed and hung
up on the line or on my wooden drying rack.
Laundry aired outside beats tumble-dried
washing hands down – sun-dried garments
exude a scent no fabric softener can mimic.
It's better for the environment, too, as well
as making your garden as pretty as a scene
from the film *Mamma Mia!*

HERE'S HOW:
Lavender Fresh

* To make a pretty posy for your washing line, gather up some stems of fresh lavender – around 8–10 will be enough. Tie a piece of string or ribbon around them at the base of the flowers to hold the bunch together and leave enough string or ribbon to make a hanging loop. Next, gently fold the lavender stems back on themselves in both directions, to form a stem 'cage' around the buds, and secure the ends together with another piece of string or ribbon. Hang the fresh lavender between the garments on your washing line.

* Vintage hankies can be used to make pretty scented pouches for your wardrobe and drawers – they make great little gifts, too. Place a mix of dried lavender, rosebuds and herbs in the centre of the hankie, gather up the edges to make a pouch and tie them securely with pretty ribbon. I used narrow neon-pink satin ribbon to tie up my sachets. Not only do they look as pretty as a picture, but they will also make your clothes smell fresh and keep moths at bay.

I ♡ dining al fresco...

THIS PAGE AND OPPOSITE This sturdy garden table and French metal chairs make for a stylish al fresco dining experience. A welcome patch of shade is provided by a decorative embroidered Indian parasol. The table has been set with mint-green glazed ceramics, ornate terracotta serving dishes and jugs/pitchers, and all the ingredients for the perfect Tequila Sunrise cocktail.

AL FRESCO DINING

MY STYLE TIPS:

* How's this for a recycling idea? Pallets are the wooden structures that support goods during transportation. Many are discarded after use, so they are readily available and the possibilities for reusing them are endless. I like to put together makeshift picnic tables simply by stacking pallets on top of each other in a higgledy-piggledy arrangement.

* Instead of always sitting in the same place in your garden, on a patio or deck, for example, find a secluded spot to move your table and chairs to, perhaps at the bottom of the garden, under a willow tree or between two flowerbeds. You will gain a completely new view.

* I love antique cutwork and white cotton lace tablecloths. For my wedding, I layered them over floral fabrics on every table. Large tablecloths can be used as bedspreads or turned into curtains, while smaller tablecloths could become a pillowcase or cushion covers. I buy mine from vintage linen shops, markets and on-line auctions. Always check the quality and condition, and if there is any damage, negotiate a lower price.

* Pots of herbs are a lovely way to adorn the table, because you can pick a few leaves to garnish your meal or add to your salad. Herbs look lovely in old terracotta pots, so keep an eye out for some next time you are perusing a flea market, second-hand shop or bazaar.

* There are so many barbecues on the market and some are very sophisticated. I prefer an old-fashioned coal barbecue to a gas one, as the cooking smell seems more intense and reminds me of my childhood. Choose one that suits your style and needs, whether it is retro-shaped, coloured or portable.

Delicious treats to enjoy outside in the sunshine...

AL FRESCO DINING

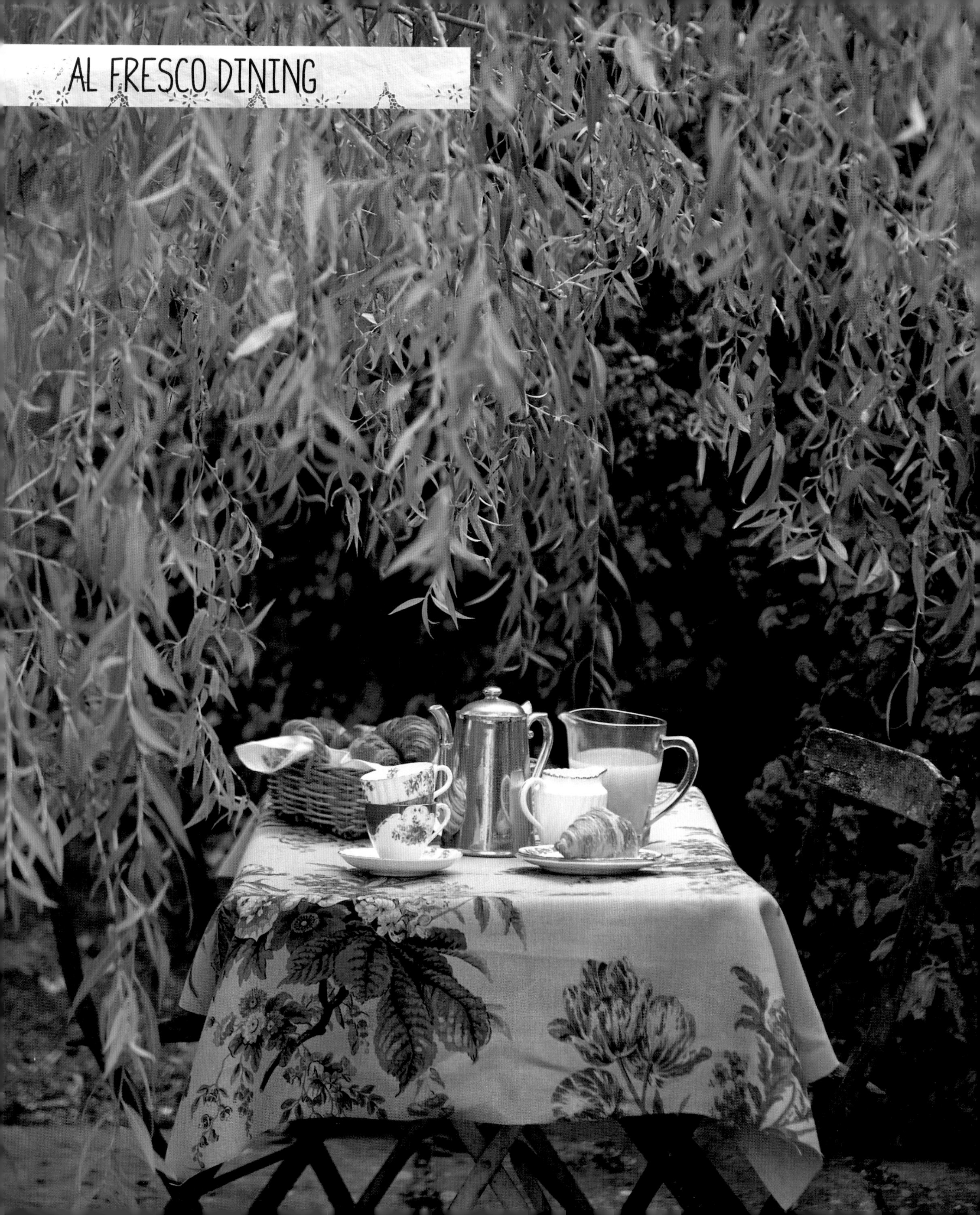

THIS PAGE AND OPPOSITE As long as the weather is good, any meal can be enjoyed outside. How about a cosy breakfast for two under the romantic branches of a willow tree, or a family lunch on the deck? Eating in the open air can be a lovely experience no matter what kind of outside space you have.

HIDEAWAYS

I love the romantic idea of a secret hideaway.
As a child, I enjoyed making dens in the garden,
in the local woods and in the cupboard under the
staircase – in true Harry Potter style! I remember
my grandfather surprising us one summer with a
lovely pastel-painted beach hut, which he had hired
for us to enjoy in Dorset on England's south coast.
That was such a special summer and I have been
fascinated by beach huts ever since. There is
something so wonderful about having a little space
to get away, where you can just sit and think or
potter and create, and it's even better if you have
a sea view. I dream of moving my home office
outside into a shed or summerhouse, and one day
I will do it. There are plenty of travel companies
offering unusual and inspirational places to stay, so
when you return home, why not recreate the look
in your shed or garage so you can be transported
far away whenever you like.

Oh! I do like to be beside the seaside...

THIS PAGE AND OPPOSITE For me, being by the beach is all about soaking up the atmosphere, collecting unusual pebbles and shells, and breathing in the salty sea air. However, the owner of this beach hut has specifically designed it for holding beachside tea parties and celebrations, as she runs her own events company, Vintage Events. Fine china is used to serve the teas and there are always lots of delicious cupcakes to be enjoyed. An array of chairs is stored inside the hut, ready for the events, and I especially love these folding chairs from the 1960s and 1970s, with their bold, cheerful patterns. This is such a lovely spot to take tea, don't you think?

Fresh, fragrant flowers make any display extra-special...

MY STYLE TIPS:

* The inside of this beach hut is decorated in a style you might not expect to see. We are familiar with the traditional nautical look favoured for seaside hideaways, but here, instead of red, white and blue, sailor's stripes and driftwood frames, there is a quirky, colourful and fun vibe. Walls are painted vivid green, while cute shelving units painted bubblegum pink hang on the walls and are used to store vintage teapots and cups and saucers.

* Next time you are at the beach and you spot a row of beach huts painted in mouthwatering sorbet and candy colours, take inspiration. Why not think about whether you could incorporate some of these pretty shades into your own hideaway or den? Valspar Paints offers an extensive array of pastel and sorbet shades from which to choose.

* Traditional deck chairs, which commonly boast a striped sling, have long been a seaside favourite, and no beach hut is ready for use until a few deck chairs have been stashed inside ready to be assembled when required. You can hire deck chairs by the day or sometimes by the hour at most seaside resorts, but they are also an ideal way to bring the seaside vibe inland, so you could always invest in a couple of deck chairs to use in your garden.

* Flowers have their place beside the seaside inside this beach hut. The hut is hired out for afternoon teas, baby showers and hen parties, so there are always vases of flowers. Use old teapots, teacups and ceramic jugs/pitchers to display flowers at home or in your own outdoor retreat.

HERE'S HOW: Hankie Bunting

✻ This is a unique alternative to regular flag bunting and is so easy to make using lots of pretty vintage hankies. I buy mine from charity shops and flea markets.

✻ Give the hankies a thorough wash before you start. Iron them flat, fold them point-to-point to make a triangle, and then simply knot each hankie together to make a chain. Keep going until your bunting is the desired length or until you run out of hankies!

I ♡ watching the world go by...

THIS PAGE AND OPPOSITE I fell in love with this Big Yellow Bus at Love Lane Caravan Park, in Cornwall on the south-west coast of England. An old American school bus has been transformed into a delightful place to stay. Some of the seats have been taken out to make room for a comfy double bed and a little table has been positioned between the remaining seats, creating a perfect spot to eat breakfast. Some of the windows have been treated to some wonderful vintage floral blinds/shades, while others have been left bare so you can admire the stunning countryside. The interior has been treated to a new chequerboard vinyl floor and the walls have been papered with vintage floral wallpaper, which adds to the uniqueness of this charming converted space.

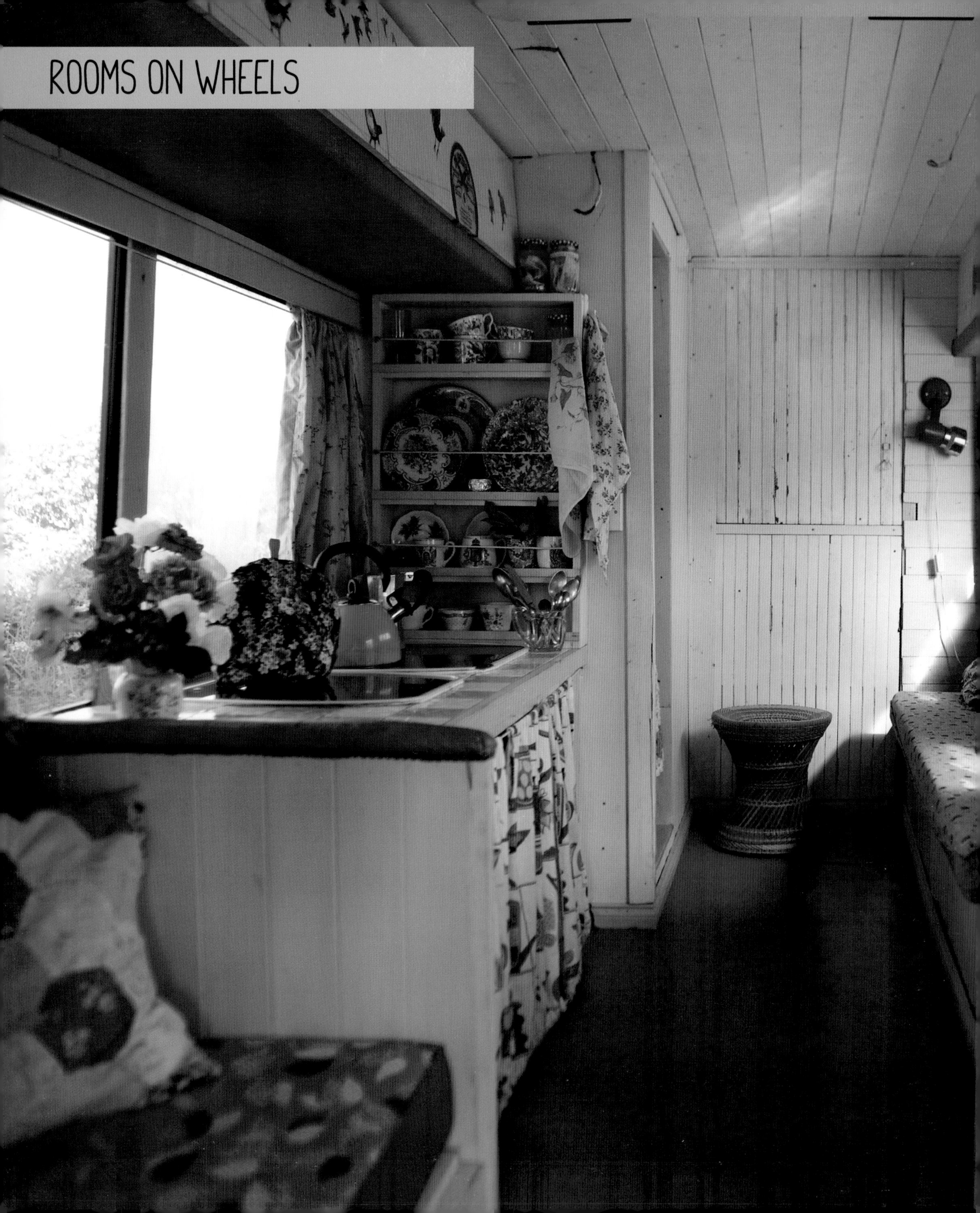

THIS PAGE AND OPPOSITE The main interior structure of this Hippie bus has been painted in pastel shades of aqua and apple, providing a good base for the riot of patterns and colours in the textiles. The bus seat pads have been re-covered in colourful mix-and-match fabrics that give the space a quirky festival feel. A collection of vintage china, vibrant melamine and old tins full of teabags are on hand for when the kettle whistles.

MY STYLE TIPS:

* To re-create the homespun style of this old bus in your own hideaway, decorate the walls in a couple of pastel shades and then go to town with bright accessories, including crochet blankets, home-made bunting and quirky printed textiles.

* Seat pads in caravans/travel trailers and motor homes/RVs can be re-covered in an array of fabrics to transform the space from plain to personal. What not take inspiration from this hippie bus and mix floral prints with bold pink woven cotton?

* Colourful open shelves make a handsome home for a collection of melamine dishes, tin plates and Royal memorabilia mugs. If your hideaway doesn't have electric or gas, invest in a camping stove and kettle.

* Double-sided curtains can be enjoyed both inside and out. Use a robust fabric with a bold pattern for the outer layer, as it will be exposed to the light and will fade.

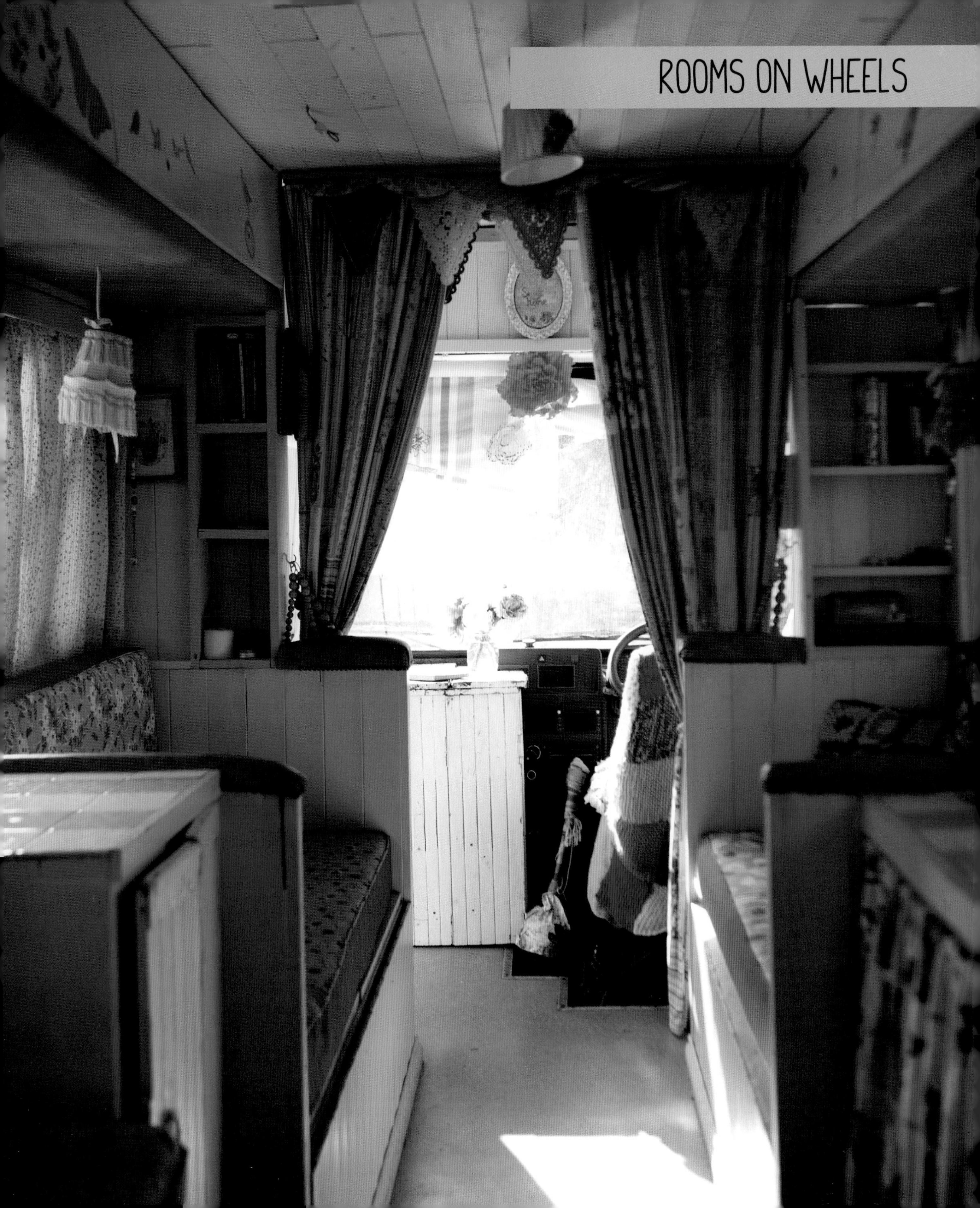

BATH HOUSE

I ♥ romantic claw-foot bathtubs...

THIS PAGE AND OPPOSITE The cute little Bath House at Love Lane Caravan Park has been made using reclaimed timber. The walls are made from old doors, the panels of which have been decorated with pretty Anna French Wild Flora wallpaper. The splash of turquoise creates a tranquil feel and the flaky paint on the side of the bathtub just adds to the charm.

BATH HOUSE

THIS PAGE AND OPPOSITE While an outside bathroom may not be everyone's cup of tea, taking a dip in a candlelit bath filled with pretty flowers inside a rustic shed is surely one of the most romantic way to have a soak – as long as there is a good supply of hot water! Treat yourself at home to a bath adorned with scented flower heads. It's a total luxury, but you deserve it.

I ♥ flowers floating in my bath...

THIS PAGE AND OPPOSITE Pretty pastel colours work well outside, and this cute little storage shed has been given a candy-stripe paint job. It looks small from the outside, but inside there is room for a barbecue, parasol, table and chairs, and a couple of sun loungers.

The walls of this outdoor shower room have been built using salvaged wooden doors and the sink base is also made from reclaimed timber. You could commission a local carpenter to build a similar structure in your garden to be used as a rustic outside retreat. Ribbon and paper bunting with a vintage floral design, such as this example from Talking Tables, can be strung up outside any hideaway to add instant prettiness.

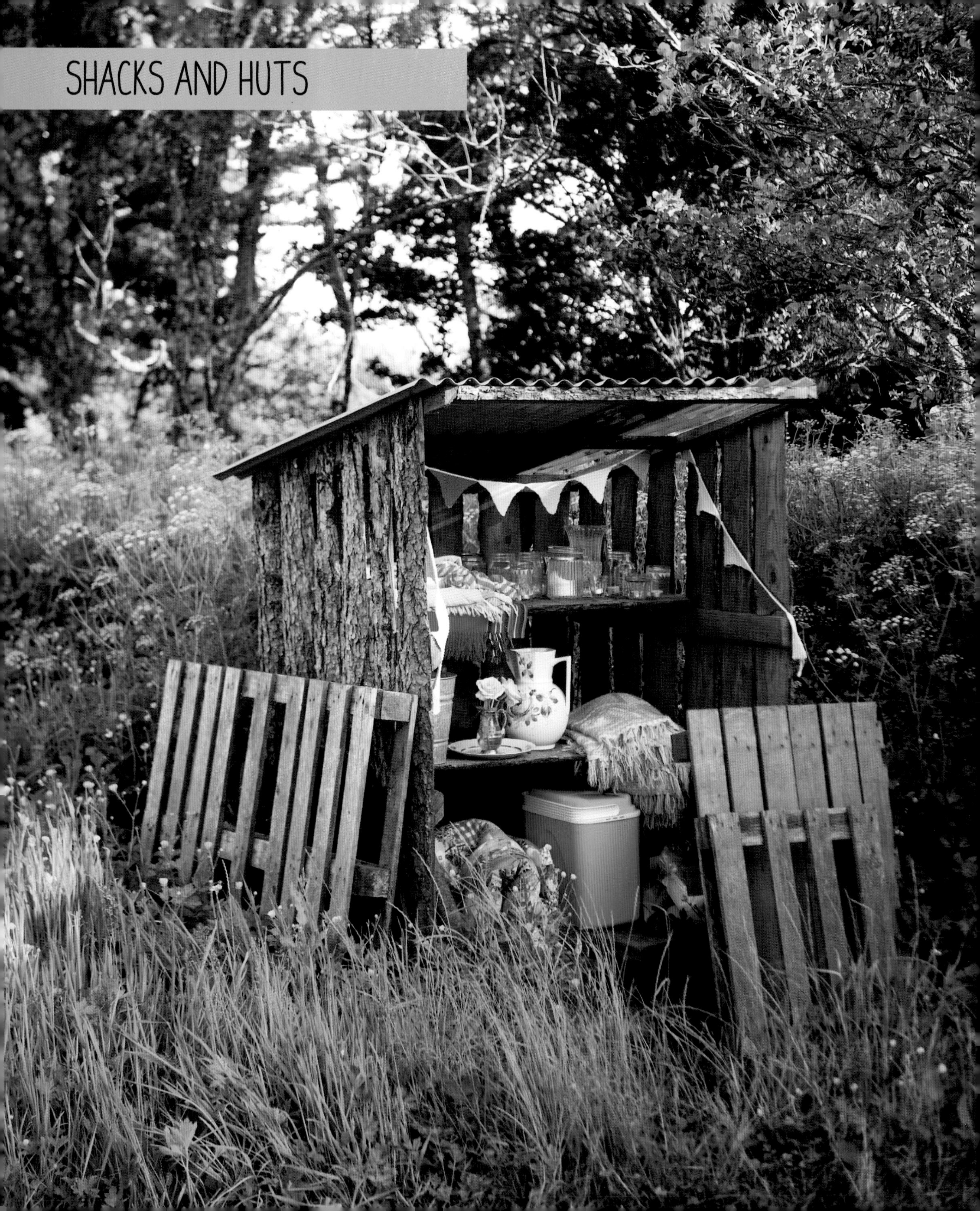

MY STYLE TIPS:

* Paint sheds and huts in pastel shades or tones that blend into the surroundings; anything too vivid will look out of place outdoors. Farrow & Ball Green Ground exterior paint is one of my favourite paint colours to use outside.

* If you are looking for a unique outdoor space to retreat to, think about converting an old vehicle or wagon, or revamping a second-hand motor home/RV. More and more people are opting to buy old vehicles, which they either transform to use in their gardens or convert into moveable business premises.

* The humble garden shed can easily become a romantic hideaway. If you cleared it out and put in a couple of old armchairs and a reading lamp, you could create an amazing space in which to work or create, tucked away at the bottom of your garden.

* Bunting and hideaways are made for each other, and any spare bunting you have can be used to decorate both the inside and outside of your cabin, shed or room on wheels.

MY STYLE TIPS:

* I absolutely love making tepees in the garden or for a day out in the park. All you need are three longish sturdy sticks, some string and a few old sheets or lengths of fabric. Simply stand the sticks up and arrange them into a tepee shape. Then tie them securely together at the top where the sticks meet using the string. Attach panels of fabric to the outside by knotting it onto the sticks. Add a ground sheet or rug and a pile of cushions, and, hey presto, you have instantly created your very own hideaway.

* For a super-stylish touch, gather a posy of fresh flowers and hang it upside down from the top of the tepee with a piece of ribbon.

* You could sew a waterproof layer onto the back of a pretty blanket to keep the base of your tepee dry.

HERE'S HOW:
No-sew Cushions

* Take a square of pretty fabric or a large silk scarf, wrap it around the cushion pad/pillow and knot the leftover fabric on either the back or front of the cushion. This works really well with round cushions.

* A glimmer of gold adds instant glamour. These ceramic beakers are by Danish brand Miss Étoile.

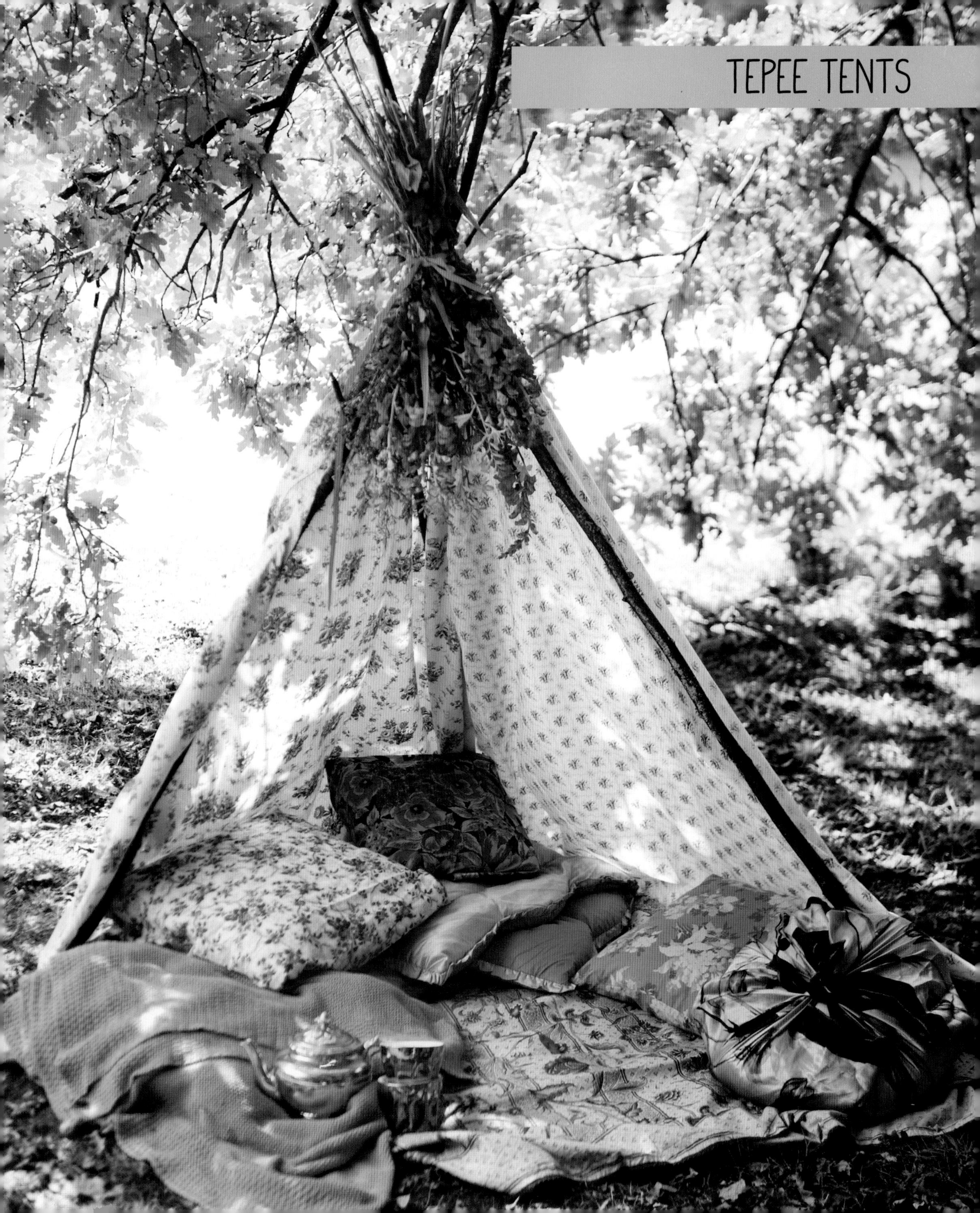

OUT AND ABOUT

Ever since I was a child I have loved going off on camping adventures. I enjoy being close to nature, sitting around a campfire in the evenings and waking up to incredible views. 'Glamping', which combines the traditional camping experience with a whole heap of glamour, is the way to do it if you don't want to forego your home comforts. There are also many unique campsites where you can book to stay in unusual outdoor spaces, from safari-style tents to canvas pods in a woodland wilderness. Getting out and about in the great outdoors, for me, always involves a picnic. I love packing up a basket with tasty treats and finding a great spot to spread out my picnic blanket. Getting out and about on my blue bicycle on a dry day is also something I love. It's great to leave my car at home, cycle into town and fill my basket with flowers from the market.

OPPOSITE This spacious safari tent is situated within Barefoot Glamping's wild-flower meadows in an area of outstanding natural beauty in Cornwall, England. This is camping on an altogether different level, with luxuries you wouldn't expect to find in the great outdoors – the tent is equipped with an *en suite* toilet and shower room, a wood-burning stove and a refrigerator. Nearby is a woodland area with a rope swing and a hammock.

THIS PAGE A deck has been built at the front of the tent and acts as a great extension to the canvas-enclosed space. It's the perfect spot to sit and take in the picturesque views. The coffee table has been made from a recycled wooden pallet with casters added to make it moveable. Before the sun sets, get some lanterns ready so you can continue to enjoy this seating area into the evening.

Home comforts and views – this is truly glamping style at its best...

MY STYLE TIPS:

* Tree-stump side tables are a great way to bring nature inside. Ask a tree surgeon for any stumps you could have and either leave them as they are or remove the bark, then sand, paint or stain them. They also make great garden stools or plant stands.

* Recycled glass jars make lovely lanterns. Just wrap wire around the rims and make a loop for hanging them. When I go camping, I always take battery-operated string lights and hang them from the top of the tent.

* The bottom right image shows a dual-purpose wall made from old crates, which separates the bedroom from the kitchen area and doubles as open shelves. This is a stylish and practical idea to steal.

* A wood-burning stove is a must for any outside space that you plan to enjoy in all weathers. This one not only keeps the tent cosy but it's also an oven!

* To ensure that camping becomes glamping, take plenty of cushions, pillows and a hot-water bottle, and pick some wild flowers to decorate the space.

CAMPING IN STYLE

Lighting helps to create atmosphere and nothing can beat candlelight...

THIS PAGE All the beds in this luxury tent have been made from old wooden pallets and dressed with simple linen bedding, velvet cushions and cosy blankets. The wall of practical shelving houses all the essentials, while the twinkling jam jar lanterns dotted around create a whimsical look, with shadows playing against the reclaimed wood surfaces.

THIS PAGE This shower room is housed in a wooden annexe attached to the back of the safari tent. It has an acrylic roof, which floods the room with natural light, a handy shelf rack with hooks and a vintage-style mirror hanging by a chain above the sink. I love the idea of using corrugated-aluminium sheets as a wall covering. It makes the room feel like a posh version of an Australian 'dunny', which you'd find in the Outback.

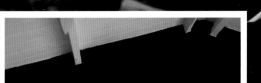

Fresh food tastes so much better cooked outside on an open fire...

THIS PAGE AND OPPOSITE Sitting around a campfire long into the evening completes the camping experience. Who doesn't enjoy sipping hot chocolate, toasting marshmallows and munching barbecued corn on the cob? At Barefoot Glamping, in Cornwall, England, there is an honesty shop where you can buy all the provisions you need for your stay – you simply list any items you have taken on the blackboard wall and pay for them when you leave. I love the idea of a blackboard wall – it's a smart, practical solution for a kitchen or home office.

I'm a huge fan of floral fabrics and love to mix and match designs...

MY STYLE TIPS:

* Bell tents are both practical and romantic and stylish. The design is simple – natural cotton canvas drapes down from a central pole and is held tight by guy ropes to create the distinctive shape outside and a wonderfully ambient space within. Quick to assemble and easy to take down, bell tents provide great accommodation for camping trips, are ideal for pitching up at festivals, create a unique party pad and make the perfect space for the kids to play in the garden.

* There are lots of lighting options, especially for bell tents, and this multicoloured tea-light chandelier takes centre stage. Each holder is filled with a battery tea light and I added some ribbon and lace streamers for a romantic look. Battery tea lights can also be placed in jam jars to make atmospheric bedside lights.

* I adore floral fabrics and I'm often drawn to floral cushions and pillowcases. Zara Home is one of my favourite sources and I also sew my own using vintage and new fabrics. I like mixing my cushions with vintage eiderdowns, which are both warm and pleasing to the eye.

* Instead of covering the floor of this tent with mats, I layered a patchwork of different Sanderson fabrics over the ground.

* This guitar, with its rose and ribbon embellishment, may not be practical for a guitarist to pick up and play, but it looks beautiful.

MY STYLE TIPS:

* A lavender field is the dreamiest place to rest and picnic. Take along a good book, a cosy blanket and a couple of cushions or pillows, and you could easily while away the day. I bought these white leather poufs at a souk in Marrakech, Morocco. They usually reside in my living room, but sometimes I take them out and about as they make great picnic seats.

* Spending time amidst the lavender, which is known for its relaxing, sleep-inducing properties, you can't help but feel calm, and the white cushions add to the feeling of serenity. Don't be afraid to use fabrics and cushions outside in case they get dirty, because if they do, you can just give them a wash and they are ready to use, inside or outside, time and again.

* Lavender and soft goat's cheese make a delicious combination, especially when eaten with fresh, crusty bread. Remember to use organically grown lavender and simply add it to the cheese board to infuse the cheese, resulting in an unusual and fragrant addition to your picnic.

* Even though most of us now have GPS maps we can use, if you have time to spare, try planning the next stop on your road trip with an old-fashioned paper map. Lay it out, close your eyes and pick a spot on the map at random to head to next. My husband and I did a similar thing while we travelled around France, Switzerland and Italy on our honeymoon.

This is the perfect spot to dream the afternoon away...

HERE'S HOW: *Lavender Bangle*

* To make yourself a gloriously scented lavender bangle, you will need some sprigs of fresh lavender, string wire and craft wire.

* Start by making a bangle shape with the string wire to fit on your wrist. Twist the ends of the string wire neatly together.

* Cover the bangle with springs of lavender, binding them in place discreetly with craft wire. Work all the way around the bangle until all the string wire is covered with sprigs of lavender.

* Make sure you fold over all the sharp ends of craft wire so that it won't scratch your wrist.

* You could make bigger versions in the same way – a garland to wear on your head, perhaps, or a wreath to hang up as a fragrant decoration.

OPPOSITE I set up this little table between the rows of growing lavender and attached a children's bicycle basket filled with blooms to the back of one of the chairs for a pretty detail.

WOODLAND PICNIC

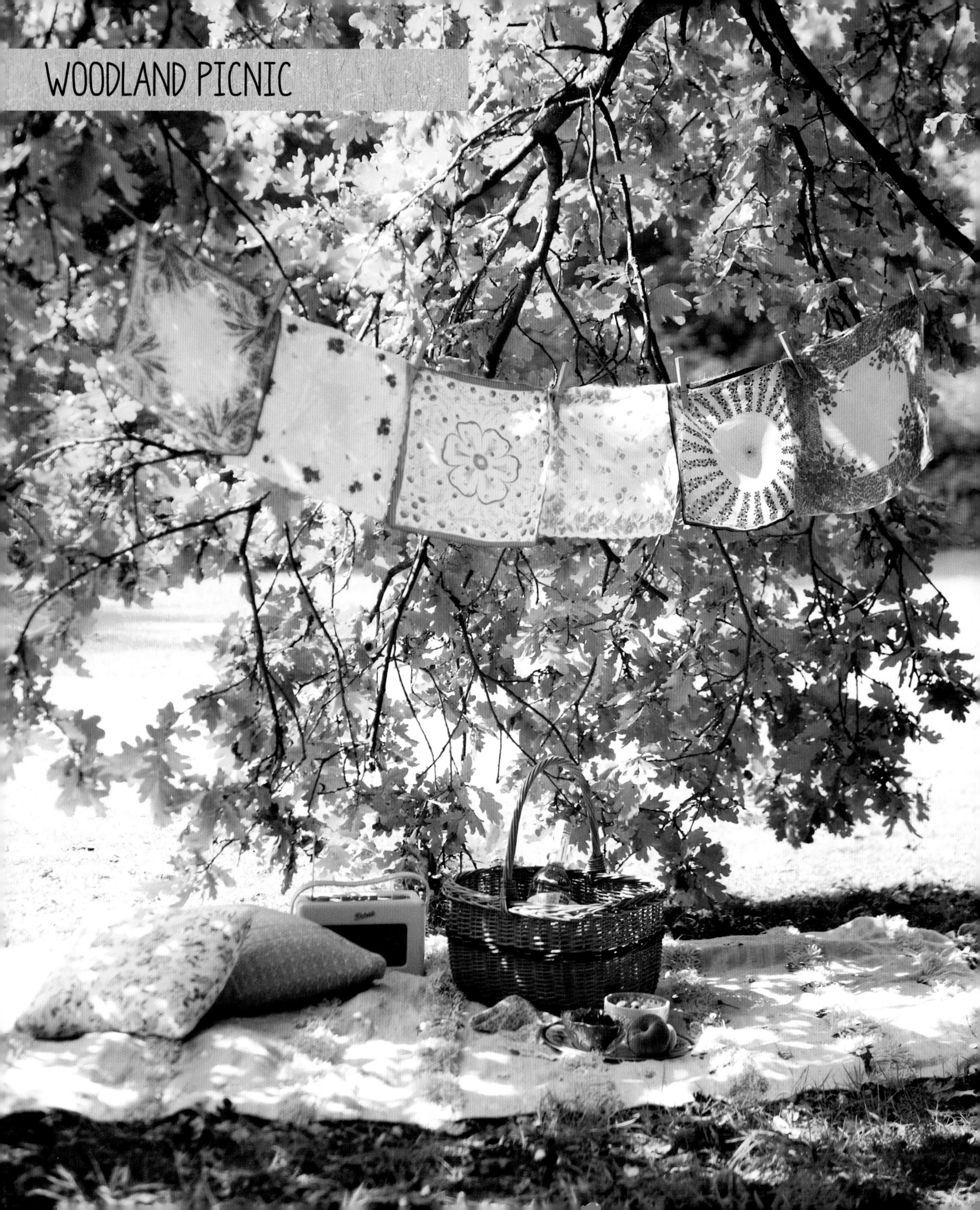

MY STYLE TIPS:

* Just the thought of a basket of edible treats to be enjoyed by your nearest and dearest in an idyllic setting is delicious. If, like me, you're a seasoned picnicker, you probably already have most of the gear you need – a basket or hamper, a blanket or mat, and your favourite snacks – but think about simple ways to add decoration to your picnic spot. A few pretty hankies, some pegs and a length of string don't take up too much room in the basket but are an adorable styling touch. Hankies are also super-handy because they can double as napkins.

* I made a charming makeshift setting under an old oak tree (see page 111) by stacking two old wooden crates together to make a table and upturning four more for stools. I covered the table in one of my favourite vintage floral fabrics and hung a handmade maypole ribbon decoration from a branch above it.

* Vintage tins are great for transporting cutlery/flatware and food, and are so much prettier than plastic containers. You can often find them in second-hand shops.

* Charity shops and flea markets are also brilliant places to source picnic baskets and wicker hampers. Look out for original 1950s hampers complete with crockery and a flask.

* Invest in a basket and rack for your bike – and even a bike rack for your car – so you can pack up a picnic, blanket and cushions, and ride off in search of the perfect lunch spot.

COUNTRY PICNIC

HERE'S HOW: *Picnic Suitcase*

✱ Old vintage suitcases from charity shops and flea markets have many uses. Here I've transformed one into a cute picnic hamper.

✱ To reline the suitcase, cut a piece of your chosen fabric to fit the base, allowing for the depth of your case and a little extra for a hem. Press the hem under all around for a neat edge, and then secure the fabric in place with double-sided tape. Repeat for the lid.

✱ Decorate the inside of the lid with bunting and tie a length of ribbon to the handle.

HERE'S HOW: *Berry Water*

✱ This is a refreshing idea to jazz up a glass of water. Simply fill a bottle with filtered water and drop in a selection of washed berries – I used strawberries, raspberries and blackberries. Place the lid back on the bottle and give it a gentle shake.

✱ Place the berry water in the refrigerator or cool-box until ready to serve. Then pour it into glasses and serve with frozen strawberries and blackberries instead of ice cubes.

THIS PAGE You can't get more 'country' than settling down to picnic in front of a tractor; just remember to ask the farmer's permission before getting too cosy. Alternatively, an old mossy bench has lots of character. It may look a little rickety, but as long as the seats are sturdy, once the checked tablecloth has been laid out, it will be a charming place to enjoy a picnic. Fresh cherries and Italian sparking orangeade make a delectable summertime snack; on the vintage tablecloth with my mix-and-match napkins, they are perfectly complemented by the colourful cut flowers.

I ♡ collecting pretty shells, pebbles and seaweed at the beach...

THIS PAGE AND OPPOSITE This is a very civilised way to picnic on the beach – folding tables and chairs are easy to transport and make picnics so much more comfortable. I painted this reclaimed folding table white and now use it often. If it's not too windy you could light some candles as the day turns to dusk and create a centrepiece of shells and seaweed to decorate the table. I jazzed up some inexpensive bunting with a few lengths of ribbon and simply pinned it around the rim of the parasol using gold-coloured safety pins, but you could always sew it on for a neater and more permanent finish. I love original folding chairs from the 1960s and 1970s with their gaudy, retro, flower-power prints.

PARTIES AND CELEBRATIONS

I've always enjoyed a good party and love
hosting my book launches, summer fêtes and
events for work, as well as casual get-togethers
with my husband and our friends. Whether you
are planning a summer party, wedding or special
dinner, taking the festivities outside can open up
a whole heap of ideas for styling and decorating.
There are lots of amazing locations outside where
you can gather friends for a party. In this chapter
I share my ideas for celebrating in country barns,
flower-filled fields, gardens and garden rooms.
It's the details that make parties
special, so check out my style tips for
dressing the table, making an entrance,
crafting decorations and creating pretty
ways to serve refreshments.

LAVENDER FIELD PARTY

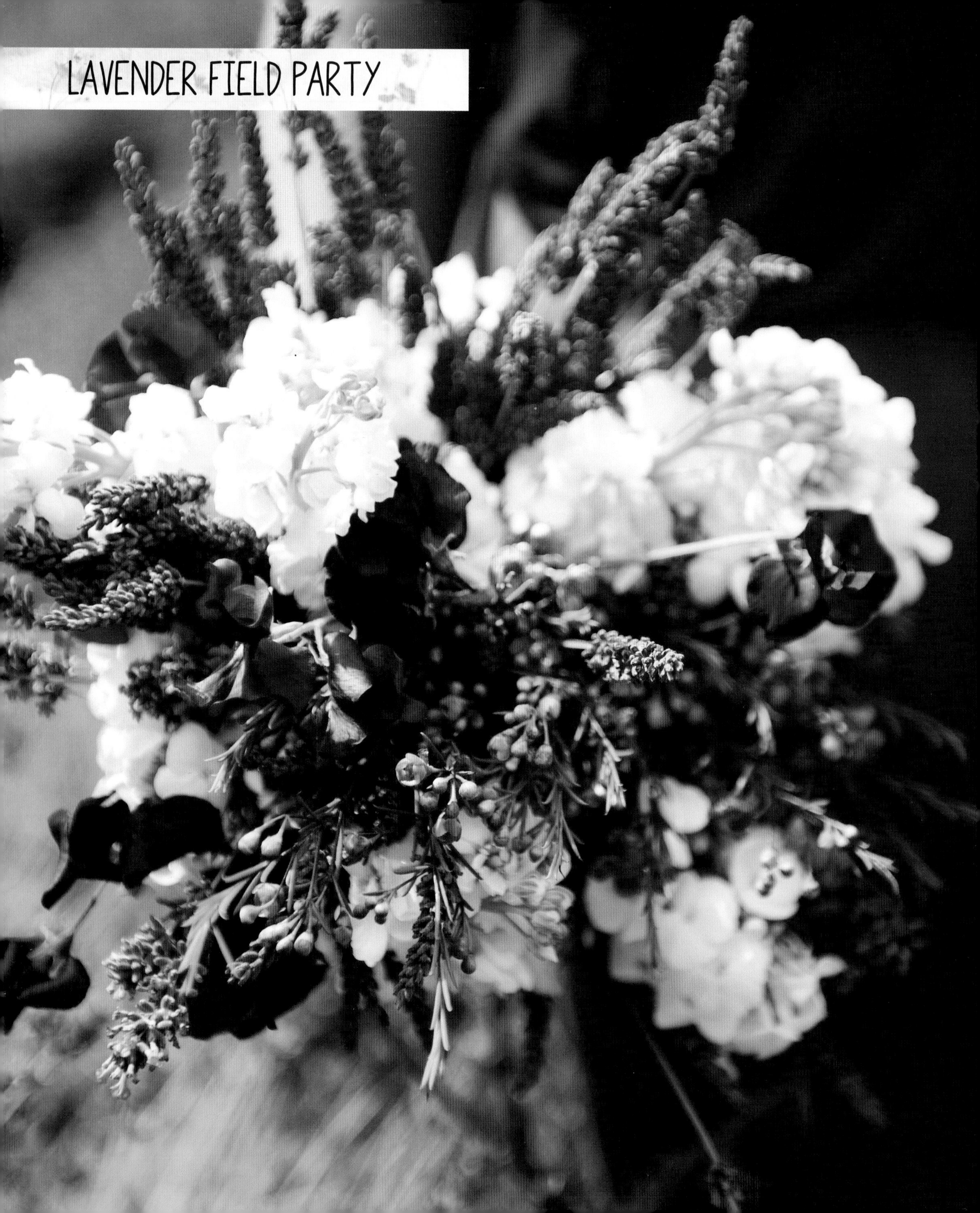

I ♡ lavender fields...

MY STYLE TIPS:

* Give a plain white tablecloth some extra style by cutting a scalloped edge around it. I chose white muslin fabric because it's light and floaty, which suited the romantic mood of this amazing setting. Use fabric scissors to cut the scalloped design. You can do this freestyle or make a card template and mark the outline with a fabric marker pen before you cut. You don't have to neaten the edges – a slightly fraying hem has a certain charm.

* Think about the colour palette of the party table or theme you are creating. I stuck to a mainly white theme with hints of heather, lavender and lilac to create a serene, romantic style. The key to getting the look right is to mix hues rather than making sure all the colours match perfectly.

* I wanted the setting itself to be the wow factor, so I mixed and matched vintage white ceramics with patterned plates in soft shades of purple.

* Decorate the table with recycled glass bottles filled with sprigs of lavender and deep purple sweet peas. I also scattered peaches down the length of the table, which add to the decorations and serve as an after-dinner treat for guests to eat.

* An absolute treat for your guests is to put together a stunning dessert table. Use a variety of cake stands to create different heights and decorate the table around the cakes with plenty of flowers. Remember to include a stack of cake plates, pile of napkins and serving equipment. If you are celebrating on a particularly warm day, position a parasol over the table to shade the cakes from the sun and cover them with glass lids to keep insects at bay.

* Cakes decorated with fresh flowers and herbs look so beautiful. My own wedding cake, made by my Auntie Linda, was a layered Victoria sponge decorated with strawberries and pink sweet pea flower heads. Sprigs of lavender look amazing as decorations on cakes; they add to the mouth-watering scent of the home-made cake and won't wilt during the course of the celebrations. I decorated this iced three-tiered cake with sprigs of rosemary and lavender – a perfect combination.

LAVENDER FIELD PARTY

HERE'S HOW: *Lavender Cocktail*

❋ Start with a measure or two of gin, depending on the size of the glass, then top up with sparking elderflower pressé and add ice. You can use champagne instead of gin or leave out both for a non-alcoholic version.

❋ Add some edible flower heads, such as violas and some chopped thyme and stripped lavender. Serve with a sprig of organic lavender and a straw. Rinse the herbs and flowers before adding them to the drinks.

HERE'S HOW: *Shortbread Hearts*

❋ Follow a recipe for regular shortbread biscuits and mix in a large pinch of organic lavender for a fragrant and tasty twist to the traditional recipe.

❋ Roll out the mixture and use a heart-shaped cookie cutter, available from most cookware or baking outlets, to cut out lots of heart shapes. Bake according to your recipe.

❋ When cool, sprinkle each shortbread heart with caster/superfine sugar and stack them on a pretty pastel vintage plate to serve. They also make lovely party favours.

HERE'S HOW: *Cutlery and Chair Decorations*

✱ Decorating cutlery/flatware for a party table is a favourite styling trick of mine. At Christmas I add berries and sprigs of rosemary to each set of cutlery/flatware and tie them together with ribbon bows. Here I used natural string and a few sprigs of lavender. I made the napkins by roughly cutting white muslin into squares.

✱ To make the chair-backs pretty, gather up two small bunches of lavender mixed with pink wax flowers and arrange them end to end, gently overlapping the stalks in each bunch. Tie the joined-up bunch to the back of the chair using a length of ribbon. Make sure the ribbon is long enough to wrap twice around the chair-back and stalks, and then tie in a bow. This is a sweet idea for the bride and groom's chairs at a wedding reception.

✱ Lavender also looks pretty worn in your hair. Tuck a few sprigs behind your ear or clip a small posy in place to adorn an up-do. If you are wearing your hair loose, make a lavender crown (see the How To for the Lavender Bangle on page 112).

129

MY STYLE TIPS:

* A long table instantly creates a special mood and works well if guests are going to be serving themselves, as they can pass refreshments and platters from one end to the other. It's easy to create an extra-long table by dragging a couple of classic wooden picnic benches together. These are available from most home and garden stores and are a great investment for the garden. Position the tables in the best spot for early evening sunshine to catch the last rays of the day.

* No party table outside is complete without flowers – the more, the better. Stems look great in a mix of jam jars and vases and I also like to scatter them on the table. Think about incorporating blooms in other ways, too – perhaps by decorating cakes with flower heads or hanging posies from tree branches using ribbon.

* One of my favourite pastimes is collecting vintage china. I simply can't resist a floral plate from a second-hand shop, especially if it boasts a rosy pattern and a glimmer of gold. Mismatched plates add a certain charm to a party table and you could team them with non-matching cutlery/ flatware for a totally eclectic look.

* Continue the mix-and-match theme with your glassware, too. When I see glasses I like, I tend to buy just two or three, instead of a set, and I now have quite a collection of assorted glasses.

* Add a few pieces of gold china or candlesticks for a touch of luxury and to reflect the sunlight.

GARDEN ROOM FIESTA

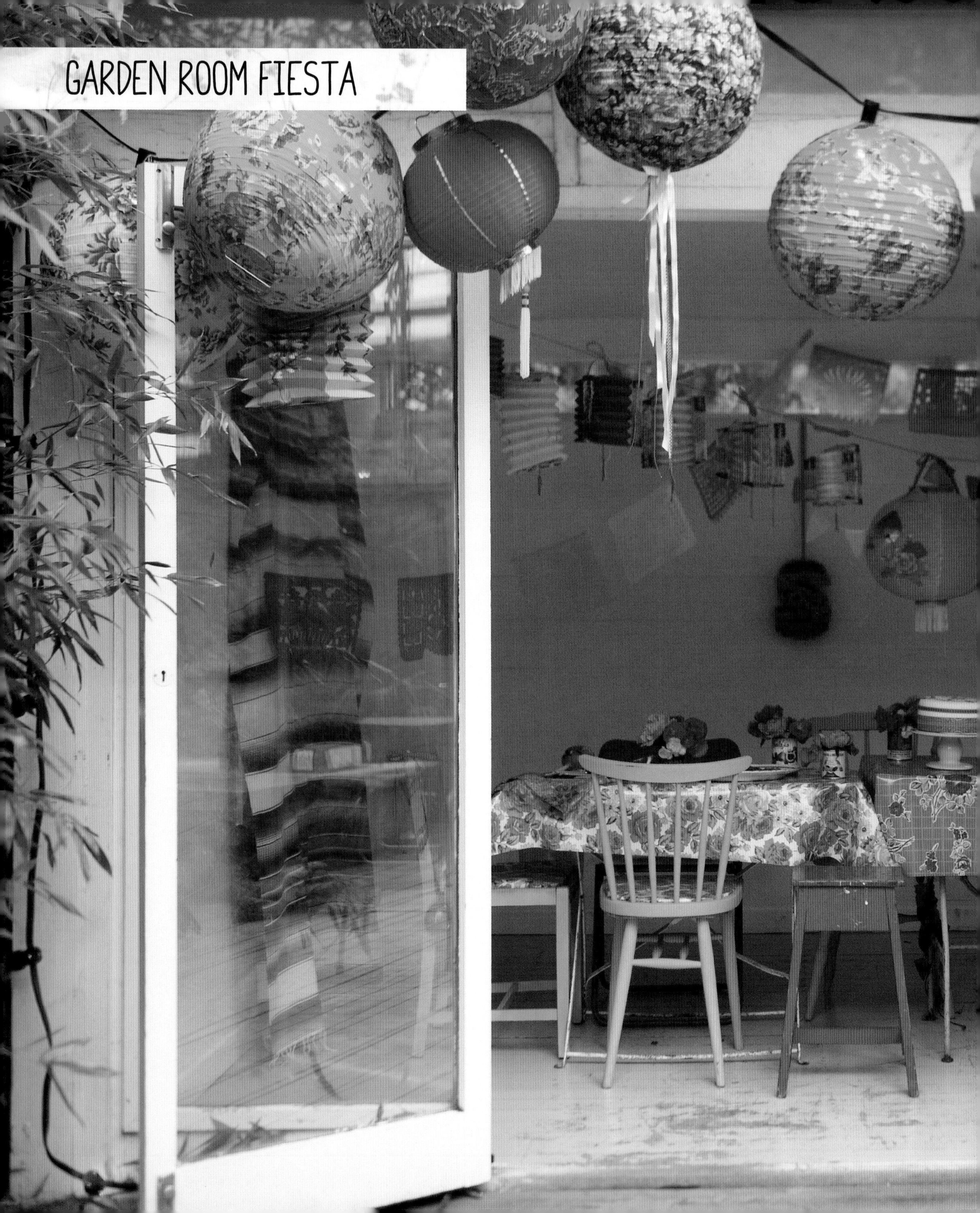

THIS PAGE AND OPPOSITE A garden room is the perfect place to hold a birthday party, as the inside/outside location works in all weathers. If you don't have a dedicated garden room, you could use a greenhouse or conservatory, or erect a small marquee in the garden. To create a fiesta theme, I used a mix of Mexican oilcloths and masses of bright, bold colours. I tied floral lanterns to a string of festoon lights outside and strung up Mexican papel picado bunting and Chinese lanterns inside.

GARDEN ROOM FIESTA

I ♥ mixing bright reds and pinks together...

HERE'S HOW: Fiesta Can Vases

✱ In keeping with the Mexican theme, I created these easy vases out of cans to display flowers. I bought a mix of food cans with interesting labels – try a large supermarket or a specialist delicatessen. Once you've used the contents, wash the inside of the cans taking care not to wet the paper labels. Fill them with fresh water and arranged the colourful flowers into posies. The cans also make great cutlery/flatware pots.

✱ The embroidered pattern on this amazing cake was made using hundreds of colourful sugar sprinkles. Have a go at this yourself (although it will take a little while!) or do as I did and commission a local baker.

Colourful ribbon is an essential part
of any party planner's kit...

HERE'S HOW: Decorating With Ribbon

✻ I keep a bag of ribbons handy so I can pull out the perfect colour whenever it's required. Cutting ribbon with fabric scissors gives the neatest edge.

✻ Ribbon is the prettiest way to hang up decorations. Here I suspended neon-pink string across the room and attached each lantern (from on-line party shop Pipii) at regular intervals with a piece of red ribbon tied in a bow.

✻ Ribbon is a great way to decorate chairs – you could attach ribbon streamers to the back of a chair or wrap a length of ribbon around one corner and tie it in a bow, as I did here.

✻ Tie ribbons around napkins and wrapped gifts.

GARDEN ROOM FIESTA

THIS PAGE AND OPPOSITE For this birthday party, the garden tables were dressed with Mexican oilcloth from Viva La Frida, which I cut to size. I then used the off-cuts to re-cover some of the old chairs, simply by stapling the oilcloth to the back of the seat pads. I completed the revamp of the chairs using a mix of green, red, pink and yellow spray paint and emulsion/latex paint. Piñatas, which are decorative papier-mâché containers that are hung up and then broken with sticks to release the sweets inside, are a traditional feature of Mexican celebrations. Make one in the shape of your chosen initial – such as that of the birthday girl or boy – and decorate it with tissue-paper fringing.

MY STYLE TIPS:

* Create a striking entrance by hanging gold and silver foil streamer curtains over an opening. I added some pastel ribbons and made tissue-paper pompoms to tie along the top. This is a romantic idea for an engagement, wedding or anniversary, and creates a unique backdrop for photographs.

* Tissue-paper pompoms are very easy to make and there are many on-line tutorials. I made some for my wedding and hung them from the ceiling of the hall where the reception was held.

* An oversize vase or jug/pitcher filled with flowers is a lovely welcoming touch. I placed this one on an upturned galvanized bucket to give it height.

* Bunting is a must-have decoration for an outdoor party. It's readily available, these days, and if you like sewing you can make your own. Hang bunting outside the venue so guests get into the party mood as soon as they arrive. I decorated the entrance to the church where I got married with white bunting.

* How cute is this tissue-paper fringe garland? It makes a sweet alternative to party balloons or banners. You could have a go at making one or support independent crafter-makers by buying their delicate handmade garlands – try Etsy, Confetti System or Scene-Setter.

* A home-made 'Welcome' sign at the entrance is a lovely way to greet your guests. You could handpaint a wooden board, use chalk on a blackboard, or cut out patterned fabric letters and sew them onto a piece of white fabric.

BARN DANCE

Why not poke fresh flowers into one corner of a hay bale?

THIS PAGE AND OPPOSITE Cowboy boots at the ready – it's time to party Western style! Empty old barns make brilliant party venues – all you need is some party lights, a few decorations and plenty of hay bales for seats. If you're not lucky enough to own your own barn, why not enquire about hiring a barn in your area or simply create a barn dance feel in your garden by buying some hay bales. I used old vintage floral curtains as tablecloths, painted a couple of wooden chairs pink and peach and added a few homesewn cushions to on old bench to make it comfy. To make the space feel welcome it made sense to open the large doors and create rows of seating ether side using hay bales. I added vintage eiderdowns and a few more cushions for comfort, while, inside, I strung up some festoon lights and tissue paper fringing decorations.Old galvanised buckets full of fresh flowers add some extra floral style.

BARN DANCE

HERE'S HOW: *Wheelbarrow Drinks*

✳ I love the idea of a moveable bar at a party.
You can wheel it around the venue, topping up
your guests' glasses as you go. It's sociable,
it looks great and it makes a real talking point.

✳ All you need is a wheelbarrow – an old,
slightly rusty one looks great but a new one
works just as well. Fill it up with ice, add
sprigs of scented flowers around the edge and
arrange the drinks with their labels showing,
so guests can see what's on offer.

HERE'S HOW: Wrapped Chairs

✱ For a different way to revamp an old chair, why not try covering it in fabric? I'm a big fan of dark floral prints, so I chose some to decorate this chair.

✱ Cut the fabric into strips and use PVA glue to stick them in place, working on one area of the chair at a time. Once the whole chair is covered and every corner is glued down, leave it to dry.

HERE'S HOW: Pink Metal Tray

✱ I found this oval metal tray in a charity shop and transformed it using Cameo Pink spray paint by Plasti-kote. You could spray an old tray any colour to suit your party theme.

I ♥ old metal trays with pretty shapes...

145

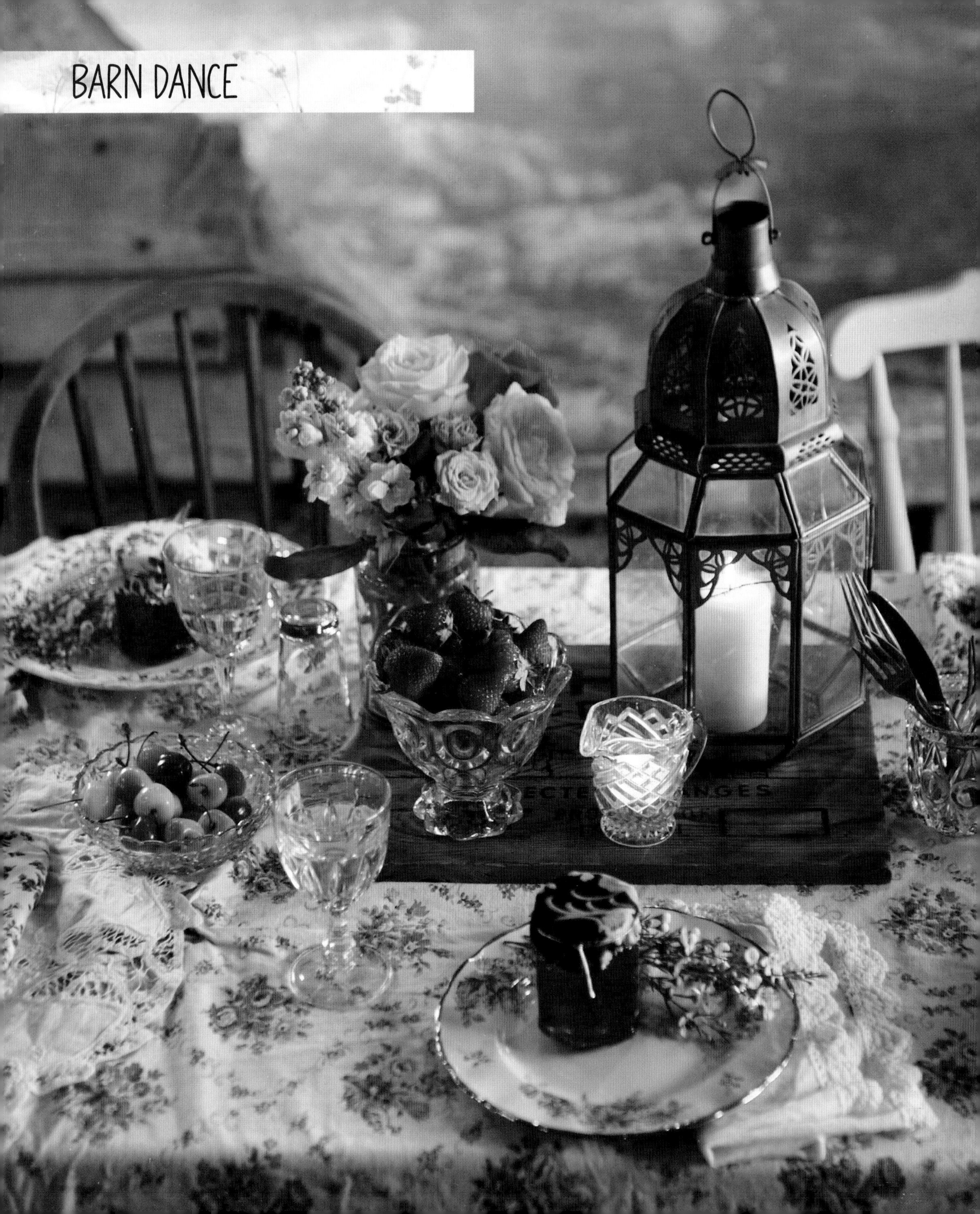

MY STYLE TIPS:

* I love buying vintage floral fabric from second-hand shops and flea markets and I often use the larger pieces as tablecloths. If you are covering a large table and the fabric you have isn't big enough to use as a single tablecloth, arrange several pieces of fabric like a patchwork to cover the whole table.

* You can always find pretty vintage cut glass for sale in thrift stores and second-hand shops. I love to give old things a new lease of life and find that cut-glass dishes and jugs/pitchers work especially well as tea-light and candle holders.

* The act of giving your guests party favours doesn't have to be reserved for weddings. I bought jars of honey from a local beekeeper and made pretty fabric lids for them. Do this by cutting circles of fabric slightly larger than the lids using pinking shears. Place a fabric circle centrally over each lid and hold it in place with gold-coloured elastic.

* Use an upturned old wooden crate as a stand for your table centrepiece.

* Borrow dining chairs, kitchen stools and office chairs from inside the house to ensure that you have enough seating for all your guests.

* If you have an accessible shelf in your venue, turn it into a bar. Position all the jugs/pitchers of drinks, stacks of glasses, cut fruits and pretty straws on the shelf. Label each jug/pitcher with a handwritten tag tied to the handle and your guests can serve themselves, leaving you free to work the room. If there isn't a suitable shelf, use a spare table to make your own bar.

I ♡ Italian ice cream...

THIS PAGE AND OPPOSITE If you're planning an event like a wedding or a birthday party, you could hire something extra special like this 1973 vintage ice cream van. Not only will it be a talking point and a lovely way to serve guests a sweet frozen treat, but it will also make a great backdrop for photos. If you don't have the space or you're on a limited budget, then why not take inspiration from Vintage Scoops and create your own ice cream parlour-themed party? Use pastel coloured decorations, dress tables with candy stripe fabric tablecloths and serve your guests ice cream in cones. There are loads of small businesses trading from unusual vehicles these days, so check online to find out what you could hire in your area. I went to a garden party once where an old Volkswagen Campervan had been transformed into a mobile cocktail bar, which was really cool!

BUTTERCUP FIELD PARTY

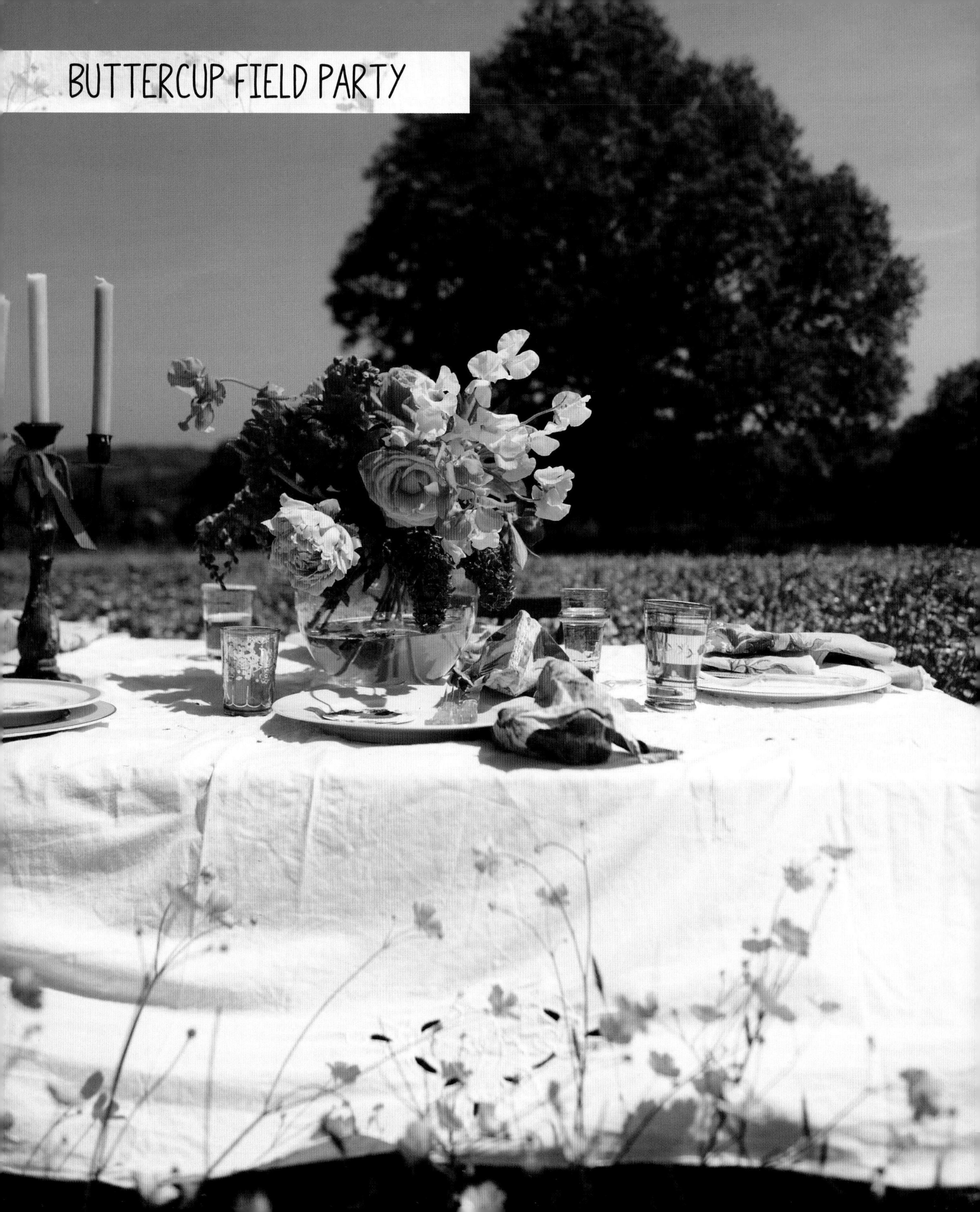

MY STYLE TIPS:

* Logistically, setting up a dining table in the middle of a buttercup field does involve a little pre-planning. Invest in a lightweight folding table that can be easily assembled and ask your guests to bring their own chairs – that way you will instantly create a casual mix-and-match feel around the table.

* If you are intending for your party to continue into the evening, remember to take plenty of candles and matches with you for when the sun goes down.

* I love decorative tea glasses, which are great to drink from and also make pretty votive candles. I like to serve special drinks in unusual glasses – there's no rule to say that buck's fizz has to be served in champagne flutes, so I use colourful tea glasses instead. Different coloured glasses are a perfect solution for parties, too, as it is impossible to mix up your glass with anyone else's.

* Flowers always transform a simple table setting into something quite beautiful. Here I used roses and sweet peas from my local florist and lilacs and peonies picked from my garden. I gathered them into posies and popped them into several glass jars and an old ceramic vase.

* I'm a big fan of colourful ceramic latte bowls, which make great little serving bowls – as here for these juicy cherries. Anthropologie stocks them in an array of colours, including this vivid yellow, which matches the yellow haze from this amazing field of buttercups.

PRETTY TABLE DRESSINGS

HERE'S HOW: *Name-Place Cards*

✽ Make sweet floral name-place cards to indicate where each guest should sit. You can also make floral-collage greetings cards, gift tags and party invitations in the same way.

✽ Cut out floral designs from fabric and giftwrap and glue them around the edges of circles of white card, using PVA glue and a glue brush. Leave space in the centre of the card to write the name of each guest.

✽ Let the glue dry completely before writing in the names and then position a card on top of each plate. I added a couple of buttercups for an extra floral touch.

I ♡ vintage florals...

HERE'S HOW: *Ribbon Bows*

✱ This simple but effective idea of tying colourful ribbons onto the backs of chairs works so well outside, as the lightest breeze makes the streamers dance. It's a cheap and easy way to create VIP seats, too.

✱ Choose your colours and tie as many ribbons to the chair back as you like, leaving long tails hanging down from each bow.

✱ I also added a neon-pink bow to the candelabra – just make sure the ribbon won't catch alight. You could add ribbon bows to vases, bottles and cake stands.

SOURCES

SELINA LAKE
Stylist & interiors author
+44 (0)7971447785
www.selinalake.blogspot.com
Twitter @selinalake

EBAY
www.ebay.com
*Online marketplace for tons
of vintage items for your
outside spaces.*

SUNBURY ANTIQUES MARKET
Kempton Park Racecourse
Staines Road East
Sunbury on Thames
Middlesex TW16 5AQ
www.sunburyantiques.com
*A great market to find furniture,
vintage plates, eiderdowns,
textiles and baskets.
(Market days on 2nd and last
Tuesday of each month from
7am–2pm)*

LIBERTY
Regent Street
London
W1B 5AH
www.liberty.co.uk
*One of London's oldest
department stores selling
innovative and eclectic designs,
with a wonderful Haberdashery
department.*

PIP STUDIO
www.pipstudio.com
*Dutch designs with bird and
floral motifs, includes textiles,
wallpaper, porcelain, stationery
and towels.*

ANTHROPOLOGIE
www.anthropologie.com
*Unique ceramics and glassware
with products sourced from
around the world; stores across
USA and UK.*

ZARA HOME
www.zarahome.com
*Pretty bath towels, bed linen,
cushions and tableware.*

OLIVE & JOY
www.oliveandjoy.com
*Online homeware store selling
designer cushions, tea towels,
furniture and more.*

HOUSE DOCTOR
www.housedoctor.dk
*Accessories, furniture and textiles
for interiors and gardens.*

BLOOMINGVILLE
www.bloomingville.dk
*Lovely designed pieces for your
home and garden*

LISBETH DAHL
www.lisbethdahl.dk
*Danish company selling pretty
glassware, candles, cushions and
accessories.*

HALFORDS
www.halfords.com
*Classic bikes including ranges by
Victoria Pendleton and Pashley;
also great for camping
equipment.*

DAVID AUSTIN ROSES
www.davidaustinroses.com
*English garden roses available as
plants and cut flowers.*

CATH KIDSTON
www.cathkidston.co.uk
*Vintage-inspired homeware,
clothing, fabrics and outdoor
living ranges.*

LAURA ASHLEY
www.lauraashley.com
*Furniture, wallpaper, fabric and
accessories.*

**VICKY TRAINOR'S THE VINTAGE
DRAWER**
www.thevintagedrawer.com
*Vintage-inspired handmade fabric
collage pieces, re-loved, re-cycled,
re-stitched, beautiful embroidered
signs, stationery and homeware.*

ROSEHIP
www.etsy.com/shop/rosehip
*Stunning handmade floral
pillowcases with crochet trims,
available in a range of vintage
floral fabrics.*

URBAN OUTFITTERS
www.urbanoutfitters.com
*Quirky home details and
furnishings with stores
throughout US and Europe.*

CONFETTI SYSTEM
www.confettisystem.com
*Beautiful handmade decorations
made with pastel tissue paper,
silks and metallic gold papers.*

BELVOIR FRUIT FARM DRINKS
www.belvoirfruitfarms.co.uk
*Delicious cordials, presses and
fruit crushes made in the
Lincolnshire countryside; bottles
feature pretty labels. Available
from most supermarkets across
the UK and US and from many
suppliers across the world.*

FRIDA LA VIVA
www.fridalaviva.co.uk
*Specialists in Mexican oilcloth
with the largest selection
available in the UK. They also
ship to Europe and the rest
of the world.*

SANDERSON
www.sanderson-uk.com
*Quintessentially English fabrics
and wallpapers, bed linen, paint
and tableware.*

THE GLAM CAMPING CO.
www.theglamcampingcompany.com
*Stylish camping and outdoor
accessories, including hammocks
and fire pits.*

FALCON ENAMELWARE
www.falconenamelware.com
*Iconic 1920s British-designed
enamelware. Check website for
stockists across the world.*

BAREFOOT KITCHEN
www.barefootkitchen.com/shop
*Cornish-based online shop
with a lovely range of outdoor
accessories.*

PAPERPOMS UK
www.paperpoms.co.uk
*Tissue paper pom poms,
fringe garlands, giant balloons
and lots more party props
and decorations.*

SCENESETTER
www.scene-setter.co.uk
*Unique party and event props
and decorations including signs,
photo booth props, crepe paper
decorations and giant letters.*

FANCY MOON
www.fancymoon.co.uk
*Fine fabrics, many with vintage-
inspired patterns.*

FOLLY & GLEE
www.follyandglee.co.uk
*Preloved and homemade items,
including crochet hangers and
bakers' twine.*

HOBBYCRAFT
www.hobbycraft.co.uk
*Arts and crafts superstores
throughout the UK.*

TALKING TABLES
www.talkingtables.co.uk
*International supplier of fun and
stylish party accessories.*

CHLOË BAKES CAKES
www.chloebakescakes.com
*Chloe bakes delicious and
beautiful handmade cakes.*

CAKEY BAKES CAKES
www.cakeybakescakes.co.uk
*Bespoke celebration cakes with
beautiful decorations and
yummy flavours.*

IKEA
www.ikea.com
*Affordable furnishings for home
and garden with worldwide
stores.*

MISS ETOILE
www.missetoile.dk
*Gorgeous homeware, party
supplies and furniture in pastel
tones and gilded gold.*

RIFLE PAPER CO.
www.riflepaperco.com
*Florida design studio producing
hand-painted illustrations and
lettering stationery and prints.*

GRANDIFLORA HOME & GARDEN
719 Grover St,
Lynden WA, USA 98264
360 318 8854
www.grandiflorahome.com
*Lovely shop selling vintage
pieces and vintage-inspired
items for home and garden.*

ETSY
www.etsy.com
*Online market place for small
businesses and craftspeople
selling homemade and vintage
items for home and garden.*

FOLKSY
www.folksy.com
*UK-based online store selling
homemade items for home
and garden.*

POWDER BLUE
3–5 Francis Street
Leicester LE2 2BE
www.powder-blue.co.uk
*Gorgeous French furniture,
romantic homeware and garden
accessories.*

LAVENDER ROOM
16 Bond Street
North Laine
Brighton BN1 1RD
www.lavender-room.co.uk
*Boutique shop selling a range of
homeware and gifts including
tea lights, lanterns, ceramics
and decorations.*

AN ANGEL AT MY TABLE
www.anangelatmytable.co.uk
*Furniture, accessories and
pretty fabrics.*

THE INDIAN GARDEN COMPANY
www.indiangardencompany.
co.uk
*Raj garden parasols and garden
accessories.*

ANNA FRENCH
www.annafrench.co.uk
*Wild Flora wallpapers, pretty lace
and fabrics.*

TINE K HOME
www.tinekhome.dk
*Danish online shop selling stylish
home and garden wares.*

DECORATIVE COUNTRY LIVING
www.decorativecountryliving.
com
*Vintage garden chairs, terracotta
pots, galvanised buckets, bird
houses and pretty plant pots.*

ROYAL DOULTON
www.royaldoulton.com
*Beautiful 100 Years of Royal
Albert collection, pretty plates,
tea cups and saucers.*

PIPII
www.pipii.co.uk
*Party decorations, picnic ware,
washi tape, pretty paper straws
and lots more.*

JUMBLED
www.jumbledonline.com
202 Anson Street
Orange NSW, Australia 2800
*Australian store with an eclectic
mix of all things wonderful for
your home and outside spaces.*

SASS & BELLE
www.sassandbelle.co.uk
*Floral fabric lanterns, ribbons and
craft supplies and quirky
cushions.*

CANOPY & STARS
www.canopyandstars.co.uk
*Unique and beautiful places to
stay and enjoy a back-to-nature
vacation including tree houses,
cabins and yurts across the UK
and Europe.*

PAINTS

PLASTIKOTE
www.plasti-kote.com
*A selection of spray paints
including outdoor sprays, which
can be used to transform second-
hand furniture pieces, metal trays
and bedsteads.*

DULUX
www.dulux.com

VALSPAR
www.valsparpaint.com

FARROW & BALL
www.farrow-ball.com

BUYING SECOND-HAND
*Search for local charity/thrift
shops, flea markets, vintage fairs,
junk shops, yard sales, antique
events, car boot sales and
auctions rooms online and in
local newspapers.*

BUSINESS CREDITS

All photography by Debi Treloar.

DAVID AUSTIN ROSES
www.davidaustinroses.com
*1, 6 background, 26, 27, 32 left, 43 left, 54, 59
above left, above centre and below right,
60–61, 65 inset above right and below right,
68, 141 above right and below right.*

BAREFOOT GLAMPING
Chymder Farmhouse
Churchtown
Nr Helston
Cornwall TR12 7BP
www.barefoot-glamping.co.uk
*7 above, 23 background 25, 98–103, 104 inset,
105 background, above left and above right.*

HELEN BRATBY
Barn and farmhouse available for location hire
near Cranbrook in Kent.
Contact: Helen Bratby
T: 01580 755 700
E: helen@helenbratby.co.uk
www.helenbratby.co.uk
*2, 6 inset, 7 below, 20 above, 44 above right
and below right, 45, 47 below left, 52 left
inset, 115, 118 above left, 119 below right,
141 below left, 142–147.*

BEACH HUT
Beach hut on Hove seafront for hire through
www.vintage-events.com
Contact: Karon Foxwell
T: 01903 879936
E: Karon.foxwell@btinternet.com
www.vintage-events.com
4, 76–79, 120–121.

HELEN AND ANDREW FICKLING
www.helenfickling.com
*3, 19, 20 below, 30 right, 31, 34–35, 38–39, 52
right inset, 62, 93 below.*

DEBBIE JOHNSON
POWDER BLUE – HOME & GARDEN LTD.
Store, props, location and styling
3–5 Francis Street
Stoneygate
Leicester
T: 0116 270 3303
www.powder-blue.co.uk
59 above right, 69.

LIGHT LOCATIONS
www.lightlocations.com
*30 above left and below left, 36–37, 42, 43
right, 70 inset, 73.*

LOVE LANE CARAVAN PARK
Roskilly's Organic Farm
Tregellast Barton
Helston
Cornwall TR12 6NX
*13 right, 14, 15, 16 right and inset, 17, 18, 21,
22, 23 inset, 74, 80–92, 104 background, 105
below right, 130–133, 141 above left.*

MAYFIELD LAVENDER FIELD
Croydon Lane
Banstead
Surrey SM7 3BE

and

MAYFIELD LAVENDER NURSERY
139 Reigate Rd
Epsom,
Surrey KT17 3DW
T: 07503 877707
E: info@mayfieldlavender.com
www.mayfieldlavender.com
66 below right, 67, 110–113, 122–129.

SARAH JANE PRALL
Waghorns
Waghorns Lane
Hadlow Down
East Sussex TN22 4EB
T: 01825 830373
E: sarahprall@btinternet.com
www.sarah-janedownthelane.blogspot.com
*Endpapers, 8–12, 13 left, 32-33, 48–51, 52
background, 53, 57, 58, 59 below left, 63,
64– 65 background, 65 inset left, 114, 119
above left, 150–151, 152 right, 153.*

DEBI TRELOAR
www.shootspaces.com
16 left, 28, 29, 134–140.

VINTAGE SCOOPS – ICE CREAM VAN
Contact: Vic and Jo
T: 01273 400416 or
M: 07758 133650
E: info@vintagescoops.co.uk
www.vintagescoops.co.uk
148–149.

With many thanks to Jacky Crisp for allowing
us to shoot her lovely home and garden.

INDEX

ACKNOWLEDGEMENTS

First and foremost, a huge thanks to my lovely friend Debi Treloar for once again capturing my styling with your amazing photography – you know I love working with you. I so enjoyed shooting this book with you, even on busy, long hot days we had so much fun that it hardly felt like work; I enjoyed our Gail's picnic lunch-breaks and car boot stop-offs too!

I would like to thank my publishers for continuing to support me and for all their hard work and dedication that went into producing this book. Also a big thanks to Barbara Zuñiga for designing this book so perfectly.

I was so lucky to shoot in some amazing locations for this book. Highlights for me were Sarah Prall's buttercup field, Helen Bratby's old barn, the Mayfield lavender field, David Austin rose garden and Love Lane caravan park. Big thanks to everyone who welcomed Debi and me into your outside spaces and let me style them up! Pippa Blenkinsop and Jess Heggs – thanks to both of you for assisting me on some of the photoshoots. Plus a huge thanks to all the shops, designers, makers and companies who sent me items I used as styling props.

Huge thanks to my blogging and Facebook friends, followers on Twitter, Instagram and Pinterest – I'd love to see some of your outdoor spaces if you've been inspired by any of my ideas in this book. @selinalake #selinalakeoutdoorliving

And last but not least to my family, who I've enjoyed many an outside picnic and party with. Mum and Dad – thanks for getting me out-and-about when I was little; I so enjoyed the trips to West Wittering beach, the picnics and adventures in Windsor Great Park and all the fun times in the garden at Crathes. Thanks to my wonderful husband Dave for taking me away on fabulous camping trips, cooking me delicious BBQ dinners and always supporting me.

♡ you x